DRIVING WITH HEART
THE DRIVING SERIES
BOOK THREE

HALEY COOK

SOUTHERN LIBRARIAN PUBLISHING

Copyright © 2024 by Haley Cook

All rights reserved.

No part of this book may be reproduced in any form or by any electronic or mechanical means, including information storage and retrieval systems, without written permission from the author, except for the use of brief quotations in a book review.

Formatting by HC PA & Formatting Services

Cover Design by Sammie Bee Designs

Cadwallader Photography

Model: Marley Williams

Editing by Steph White (Kat's Literary Services)

Proofreading by Louise Murphy (Kats Literary Services)

ISBN: 9798343895353 (Paperback)

ISBN: 9798343895506 (Hardback)

DRIVING with *Heart*

HALEY COOK

To all those little girls out there who think they can't go the same speed.

Think again. You have the heart of a warrior.

Chapter 1
Mila

Deep breath, Mila, you can do this...

Over the last few days, I may have freaked out a lot with the announcement, but it's here, and I can do it. It's not like I haven't talked to the press before, and Grace will be right by my side in case I sound like I have no brain, which, by the way, as I am standing here staring out at the reporters, may just be the very case. Taking another deep breath, I try to give myself yet another pep talk just as Grace, my PR guru, comes up.

"Hey, you okay?" Grace asks with a concerned look on her face. Guess she can see that I'm having an internal freakout right now as well. Over the course of the last six months, she has become one of my best friends. And I can't imagine anyone else with me during this exciting and terrifying time.

Taking yet another deep breath, I turn to face her, and I know she can see the intense worry written all over me.

Grabbing my hands in hers, she squares her shoulders and goes into PR mode for just a second to help me calm down before I throw up all over her red-sole heels.

"Mila, look at me."

I lift my eyes to meet hers.

"You are a badass driver. You are ready to show this boys' club just what you're made of. Do you understand me?"

Shaking my head to bring myself back into the moment, I

know that I'm a capable race car driver. I've proved that to anyone who has questioned me since I was sixteen years old. I can handle the boys' club that I'm about to step into. Even though I'm terrified of the intense microscope that is going to be on me, I also know that I need to do this for all those little girls watching the sport and thinking, "If she can make the jump, so can I."

Running my hands over the white blouse I had spent far too long ironing, I comb my hands through my dark hair one last time before giving her a firm nod.

"Okay, let's do this then."

I watch Grace step onto the stage to speak with the press and answer a few questions. "I would like to introduce the newest member of the Mac Motorsports team. I'm sure some of you have already heard the buzz around this person, and we couldn't be more excited to have this amazing female driver on our team."

"Mila Michelson."

I hear my name come over the speaker and know it's time to put on my practiced smile and face the firing squad.

Stepping up to the podium, I can't help but wrap the paper sitting on it in my hands. Grace had left it for me to read so that I didn't sound like a complete idiot while talking because I can ramble when I get nervous around people. Put me in a race car going two hundred miles an hour, and I'll drive the hell out of it. But put a mic in my face, and it's like I have no filter.

"Hello, everyone. I just wanted to start by saying that I am beyond grateful for this opportunity to be a part of Mac Motorsports. Being teammates with Ryan McKenzie and Matt McCall, I couldn't have asked for a better atmosphere and welcoming into their world here. It truly is a family when you walk these halls. I'm excited to show what I can bring to the table and hopefully give these boys a run for their money. Being in NASCAR has always been my dream since I first got into a midget car at sixteen years old. So, to be here today, standing in front of you, I am in awe of how far I've come. Granted, at twenty-three, it's not been a long ride, but it's been great so far, and I can't wait to see what is to come this season. The yellow stripe is a rite of passage, and I intend to prove I'm able to play with the big dogs."

"So, hold on tight, and to all the girls watching this, go out and get in that car and make your own way."

Grace steps back up to the mic as I finish my speech.

"Mila will take just a few questions before we get back to work preparing for next season," she states.

- Reporter Mike John, PRN: "Mila, do you think you're ready to go head-to-head with some of the greats of this sport?"

"Well, John, I think when it comes time to race, the only thing that matters is can I race them? Yes, I get I'm a female, and it's a male-dominated world, but just because I pee sitting down doesn't mean I can't drive a car just as hard as any man out there."

- Reporter Jason Goins, MRN: "Mila, coming to Mac Motorsports, are you ready to be a part of a team, and how was it meeting the two other drivers in this organization?"

"The team has been great. Both Ryan and Matt have been very welcoming and have helped me over the last few months get used to the new car that we will all be driving this coming season, making me feel like I'm a part of this family they already have. I can honestly say I had a few options for teams for this season, but when I came to see the setup at Mac, they acted like I was already a part of the team."

"Okay, that's all for today, guys. Thank you again for coming, and we look forward to watching Mila in action come February at Daytona Speedweek."

Walking off the stage, I finally let out a long breath and relax.

"Mila, you did so great up there," Grace says, coming to stand beside me.

"Thanks so much for staying up there with me. I don't know

why they make me so nervous. It's like I forget how to talk sometimes."

"Girl, you did perfect. I would have never known," she says as she looks around the room.

"Who do you keep looking at? Ahh, never mind. I see a certain blond playboy in the corner trying to hide but not doing a great job at it," I say as I give her a nudge in that direction.

"Ex-playboy, and come next week, he will be my husband." She gives me a wink.

"I'll see you at the wedding," she adds right before giving me a hug and walking toward Matt, who then dips her for a kiss, making all the media go crazy.

Shaking my head, I head out of the media room and to the crew halls.

This is gonna be one hell of a ride, and I just hope I can handle all that comes with it. It's what I have wanted for so long, and now it's here.

Chapter 2
Chase

"There's my favorite patient."

"Son, I'm your only patient this morning, so I think that's a given, isn't it?" Mr. Sims announces to no one as I round the corner to get started on his therapy.

"Yeah, maybe you're right, but you're also my most cranky one of the day if we want to split hairs."

"Well, son, someone has to keep you on your toes, or you'll be bored to death with just us old people when the pro athletes aren't here to keep your attention," he points out.

"Alright, let's see what you got today then. Let's get you on the table and check that knee out."

Sports medicine has always been a love of mine. From the time I could take the intro class in high school, I knew what I wanted to do, and here I am, six years later, working at one of the top sports medicine clinics in Charlotte, NC.

Granted, yes, we work closely with a lot of the major sports teams in the area. It's the older guys who come in that I enjoy the most. They're the ones who like to bust your balls because you're not dressing a certain way, and their tales of "Well, when I was your age..." are the highlight of the workday.

"Chase, when I was your age, I already had a wife and two boys running around. Seems like you can't even go out on a date without that phone attached to you," Mr. Sims spouts to me as I check his knee out. He's been coming here for four weeks now after a total knee replacement, and it's always the same thing.

"Chase, did you do anything this weekend? Any lady friend I need to meet? Son, are you into men? Because I'm okay with that." The same three questions each Monday morning. And my response is always the same—nope to all three.

Shaking my head, I can't help but laugh just a little at him, thinking back on my days at App State. It was easy to meet girls and talk to them, but also women were everywhere. Now, I fill my days with work and then go home to my golden retriever, Miller, truly living the bachelorhood life.

The one weekend I stepped out of my comfort zone and went on a blind date ended with me competing with none other than Ryan freaking McKenzie. Who the hell can compete with a pro athlete? Tinley was a drop-dead gorgeous, soft-spoken bookworm. We had a ton in common, and I really thought we might have had a connection, only to see a picture of her later that weekend kissing Ryan. So that ship sailed quickly. And honestly, I just haven't made time for a relationship since then.

"Son, are you even listening to my story?" I hear Mr. Sims say as I pull myself out of my fog, thinking of Tinley.

A blush creeps onto my face just a little, as I know I've been caught not listening to the man.

"Sorry, Mr. Sims, I kind of drifted off for a second." I laugh to myself.

"Son, what girl made you have that faraway look just now?"

Shaking my head, I say, "Just an old memory from college that feels like a completely different life now."

After getting Mr. Sims ready on the bike to stretch out his knee, I make my way over to the coffeepot and pour myself a generous amount. If my mind is already wandering, I'm gonna need a few of these. What in the hell has gotten into me today? It's been a long time since I've even thought about Tinley. And now she pops into my head like it was yesterday.

An hour and a half later, I watch as Mr. Sims heads toward the exit and hear my name being called by my boss, Jasper. The man is in his late fifties and has that deep rasp in his voice, letting you know you don't want to be on his bad side. Well, that and him being built like a twenty-year-old. If it wasn't for the gray hair, you might guess we were the same age.

"Hey Jasper, what's up?" I ask, walking into his office. Pushing the chair out from the desk to sit in front of him, I drink my coffee as he talks.

"Chase, I need you to create a workout and nutrition plan for a local race team we just took on as clients. They have three drivers. We just need to make them something easy to follow on days they aren't at the race shop, as we will be with them when they are back here during the week," he says.

"Umm, okay. When do you need me to get this together and head over to meet with them?"

It's not uncommon for our office to work with race teams on workouts and their eating habits, but normally, they have an in-house person to do that. But Jasper has been trying to expand more into this environment for a while now.

"Actually, you can head over there now. They're expecting you. Mac Motorsports is the client."

Son of a bitch, of course that's the team it would be. Well, guess it's time to face the guy who got the girl, and I just thought that the old memories were that—old. But now it's going to be right in my face.

After taking the long way around to get to the race shop, I pull up to the gate of Mac Motorsports, give my name, and then I'm directed to where I need to go.

Grabbing my bag out of the back of the car and pulling on my hat, I head toward the workout facility to get this day over with.

As I walk into the workout room, I notice some of the crew

guys already in mid-workout on the treadmills and lifting weights. Damn, these guys are huge for pit members, but I guess with having to throw tires around for three or four pit stops a race, they have to be.

Placing my bag down on the nearest table, I grab my laptop and get the program up and running, which we use to set out our nutrition and workout plans for clients.

While engrossed in the task at hand, I am oblivious to someone approaching me until they clear their throat. Looking up from my computer, I face none other than Ryan McKenzie.

Ugh, does the universe have something out for me today? The man smirks at me when I finally make eye contact.

"Chase Bryant, what a surprise to see you here. Of all the sports medicine guys they could have sent, you come to my team," Ryan says with that smile that never leaves his face.

"Ryan McKenzie, been a while, man. Guess you're doing good. Saw you and Tin got engaged a while back."

Take the high ground, Chase. Not that you're still over here pining for the girl who you never had a chance with.

Reaching his hand out to brush his hair back, he says, "Yeah, she's the best thing that's ever happened to me."

Well, this isn't awkward at all, I think, scratching the back of my neck.

"Well, if it isn't Chase Bryant." I hear an all-too-familiar voice come from behind me.

Turning around, I see Grace Miller walking toward me. This day just keeps getting better.

"Grace, great to see you," I say, trying to make it seem like just another day.

"Heard you got married a few weeks ago. Congratulations to you and Matt. Gotta say it was entertaining watching it play out in front of the cameras. Only you would have been able to tame the playboy of NASCAR, as the press likes to label him."

Laughing, she smiles at me. "Oh, you don't even know the half of it, Chase." Then she looks over my shoulder just as Matt walks in the door.

"Well, if everyone is here, let's get to work, shall we?"

Chapter 3
Mila

My gosh, how in the hell did I sleep through my alarm? Putting my car in park, I jump out and race toward the workout room.

Of all the days, today, I needed to be on time. I wanted to make a good first impression with the team and my teammates. Yet here I am, racing down the hallway like a teenager late for class. I guess, in some ways, I feel that way. I'm the rookie, the new kid in town. The token female driver in a male-dominated sport.

Matt and Ryan have been in the sport for a few years now. They have an unbreakable bond, and now, here I am, being launched into the middle of their bromance. Granted, I have had a little help learning that, with Grace giving me some inside information on their dynamic. Over the last few months, she has become such an amazing friend, and getting to know Tinley helped my transition to North Carolina so much; it's as if I was always supposed to be here.

Bursting through the door, my clumsiness gets the best of me, and the next thing I know, I'm tumbling ass over head, landing face-first in front of Matt, Ryan, and Grace. *Fuck my life.*

Yep, I'm just going to lie here. Just leave me. Nothing to see here, folks. I laugh, throwing my hands up in the air.

"Care to grab my hand and let me help you up, my lady?" I hear a deep timbre voice come from above me.

"Nope, I'm good. I just need to stay here a little longer." I'm not sure my pride can take me tripping over anything else.

"Well, I think you've been on the floor long enough; again, let me help you," that voice says again with a little laugh behind it.

Rolling over, I'm hit with the most beautiful sea-glass green eyes I think I have ever seen.

Holding his hand out, I finally get off the floor.

As I stand up, I realize everyone is, of course, staring at me. I mean, why wouldn't they? Not only was I late for an important team meeting, but then I stormed in like a bull in a china shop and fell flat on my face. Unfreaking believable, that's how my luck goes. *You just can't go in and be graceful, can you, Mila?* I want to smack myself in the forehead.

Looking back at the man with the sea-green eyes, dark-blond hair that I want to run my hands through, and a small dimple that I notice, I find him looking at me as well.

I reach my hand out to him. "Hi, I'm Mila Michelson. The newest member of the Mac Motorsports family and all-around clumsy woman," I say with a small laugh.

"Hello, Mila, I'm Chase Bryant," he says, reaching out to shake my hand, sending a strong electric current up my arm.

Smiling up to him, I hear a throat clear behind me. I turn and see Grace coming up to me.

"Mila, you really know how to make an entrance, don't you?" Grace says, laughing as she gets closer, with Matt and Ryan following behind her in tow.

"Well, you know I'm nothing if not a good time," I say, winking at Chase as I turn around to greet Grace.

Chapter 4
Chase

Well, this day just got a lot better. Watching this drop-dead gorgeous, raven-haired beauty face-plant in the middle of the gym brought out my knight in shining armor, wanting to make sure she was okay.

I mean, you would have thought her ass was on fire the way she came bursting through the front door. I also couldn't help but feel a pull to her in that instant.

After letting her lie on the floor for a few minutes, as she had instructed, I finally coaxed her up off the floor, and the small contact with her made goosebumps break out along my skin.

"It's nice to see the last member of the team is here," I say, getting my wits about me so that I can get the assessments underway and see what needs to be done for the workout and nutrition plan.

Ryan is the first to have a seat in the chair. Of course, he is the golden boy of the team. Ugh, why do I still feel like I have something to prove to him? *Move the fuck on already, Bryant. It was over before it even began.* Shaking my thoughts away, I get on with the day.

THE TEAM BREAKS for lunch just as I finish up Matt's assessment. The man has the physique of Thor and speaks with a Southern accent, so I knew it would be easy enough to get his workout plan going. And having Grace make sure he sticks to the nutritional plan was easy enough. That woman has him by the balls, and I couldn't help but laugh just a little at the side-eye she gave him or the sass leveled at him when he wanted to object to certain things.

Just as I'm finishing up putting in my notes for Matt, I hear a throat clear in front of me. Pulling my glasses off, I see the dark-haired beauty in front of me.

"Well, I guess it's my turn," she says, pulling the chair out from behind the table to sit across from me.

"Guess so. Um, I'm Chase. Officially, this time," I say, reaching my arm out to shake her hand one more time.

"I'm Mila, officially. Sorry for the dramatic entrance this morning," she says with a small smile and a hit of pink on her cheeks.

"I'd say that was one way to get the room's attention, that's for sure, Mila." Smiling back at her, I can't help but notice the minor details of her face. The way her dark chocolate eyes track me as I talk, or the way her perfect mouth curves at just the right angle. *Get it together, Bryant. She's the client. That means off-limits.*

Shaking my head to clear my thoughts, I hear a faint laugh come from her, and, of course, my dick wants to join the party now. *Son of a bitch, get it together.*

"Okay, so the plan for today is to figure out where you are physically so that you have plenty of stamina in the race car to drive not only the short half-mile race tracks but the super speedways and the road courses without burning yourself out or suffering from heatstroke once you get out of the car after the race."

"Oh, Chase, I can tell you already. I have plenty of stamina." She says this with a smirk, and my dick takes notice.

"Well, that's good to know, Miss Michelson," I say, throwing right back the innuendo I know she meant to do. She wants to play the part of the siren calling to men, then hell, I'll let her. It's been too long since I let the beast out to play, and if she wants to go down this road, even for just a little, I'll let her.

"Let's head over to the treadmill and see how you fair on it, shall we?" I stand up with a smirk and motion her over to the machine.

Adjusting myself as we go, I set the treadmill at the speed that I need to do her assessment and then wait for her to start.

When I look up at Mila walking toward me, my tongue nearly falls out of my mouth. Dammit, the woman has stripped out of her baggy clothes and is now wearing the tightest leggings I have ever seen and a sports bra that shows just how amazing her breasts are. Well, talk about not playing fair, but hell, if she wants to walk around like that, showing off that beautiful body, who am I to object? Especially since I get a front-row seat to it.

Grinning at me just a little as she walks over to the treadmill, she says, "What's the matter, Mr. Bryant? Cat got your tongue?"

If you only knew what this tongue wanted.

I clear my throat as she steps onto the treadmill.

"Okay, so we are going to do a ten-minute assessment. Every two minutes, I will turn the speed up, and if you feel you need to slow down or stop, let me know."

"Like I said before, Chase, I have plenty of stamina. So you can push me to my limit. Do I need a safe word?" she says just as she starts to run.

Chapter 5
Mila

This day just took a turn, and I am all here for it. When Grace told me we had to have a physical exam with a trainer and nutritionist, I thought today was going to suck balls—some old man looking to torture us and make me feel bad about having a burger instead of salad. But the second this gorgeous guy helped me off the floor, my entire outlook changed. And the sass that I bring to everyone I meet came out in full force.

I had planned to just keep my baggy clothes on during my workout, but when he flirted just a little with me, I couldn't help but let my inner siren come out to play. And here I am, running in just my sports bra and leggings. If I had left my T-shirt on, then I would have missed the hot-as-hell face I received from Chase when he finally looked up from his clipboard. I gotta say, I never thought glasses were sexy until I saw them on this man. I like the whole Clark Kent vibe he's giving off.

I know I'm toeing the line here with being professional, but when the heavens send you this specimen for a treat, you can't help but play along.

Starting my run, I try to keep my focus on the task at hand and not get distracted by Chase. The very last thing I need is to get hurt trying to look cute and flirt with him. After five minutes of running on this damn thing, I think he's just torturing me, and I'm about to go into another pit of hell when he comes to stand in front of me. Dammit, now I can't look at him.

"You weren't kidding about the stamina, Michelson. I was at least expecting you to give me a little attitude about the run," he says while writing something on the clipboard.

Just when people think they have me figured out, I throw a curve and surprise them. That's been my go-to for as long as I can remember. From an early age, I knew I differed from the other girls. I didn't have the desire to play with dolls or become a Disney princess. I wanted to make my way in the male-dominated sport and show them I belonged. I wanted the road less traveled because it was hard. So I've worked my way up to this spot, and I'll be damned if I'm going to let anyone come between me and that checkered flag.

Finally, after ten minutes, my legs feel like jelly as I step off the machine and find Chase waiting at the next one, grinning like the cat that ate the canary.

"You know you're getting a little too much pleasure in watching me suffer right now, right?"

"Oh, I'm just getting started with you, sweetheart. Do we need to go back to the safe word conversation again?" he says, putting his glasses back on with a cocky grin.

"No, sir," I say with all the sass I know he wants and walk toward the next challenge.

After the machine from hell, I'm ready to throttle Chase and his smug face. He made me row for what felt like forever, and he took pleasure in seeing me grimace during the final two minutes.

Standing up, I really felt like my body was going to keel over. I don't think I have worked out this hard in a long time, and that might be why I'm pushing myself like this. Because I know I need to be at this level of dedication.

"Alright, that's enough machines for now, Mila. Let's have a seat and figure out what you're eating." I follow him over to the table he has set up with all his computers and a tablet.

"You know that telling a woman what she can or can't eat

goes against a lot of things, right?" I say, laughing as we walk back.

"Not when you're being paid to be in top form, and you're expected not to suffer any ill effects every time you step out of the car because you went out and partied the night before. This isn't the era of the Yarboro's anymore, and the good ole boys' club isn't what it used to be," he says very matter-of-factly.

"I'll have you know I only party when the race is over. During the week, I take eating and drinking seriously, and that may be the least of your worries about my plans. As a woman, I know my looks get me places. I'm not naïve about that. So I make sure this ass looks good from all angles."

Smirking up at me from his computer, I can't help but feel the pull to get to know this man a little better. The only problem is that we work together, and I make sure that I don't cross that line. I want no one to think I got where I am by sleeping my way up.

"Gotta say, Mila, you have done an excellent job of keeping that ass pretty top-notch. The workouts are simple for you, honestly. Treadmill, some light weights, and rowing are all you need to focus on. Make sure that you are getting in at least an hour a day on race weeks, and on the weekends, you can just do a jog around the infield to get your muscles warmed up before getting in the car. For food, make sure you have a lot of protein on hand during the weekend. The weekly meals, I would say just to be conscious of what fats you're eating. But honestly, just looking at you, I'd say you know what you can and can't eat," he says as he types in his computer before sending it over to my crew chief and Grace.

"Thanks for helping with this, Chase. It was nice to meet you. I'm sure I'll be seeing you around the shop at some point. And who knows, I might need some extra instruction on my workouts." I wink before reaching over to grab my shirt and heading toward the door, making sure I put an extra sway in my hips.

When I look over my shoulder before pulling the door open, I notice Chase pulling his glasses off that gorgeous face with a smile and shaking his head.

Chapter 6
Chase

Talk about an interesting day. Once I packed up all my stuff and headed out, I couldn't wipe the smile off my face. Mila was drop-dead beautiful, and that body was one that men only dream of. She had curves in all the right places, and I knew without a doubt she was going to be starring in some very dirty dreams later.

I head to the clinic to check in with Jasper and give him the rundown of the day with Mac Motorsports. I am ready for the day to be over and to go home to my dog and a beer.

Pulling the door open to Jasper's office, I can't help but smile at the man who has a permanent scowl on his face. Jasper was in the Air Force before finishing up his time with the very famous Blue Angels. Now he finds himself behind a desk and pushing paperwork five days a week. Gotta say, some days, civilian life doesn't suit him, but he may be content.

"If it isn't Mr. Pain-in-my-ass, Chase Bryant," he says with a laugh as I come to sit across from him.

"Looking like hell today, Jasper," I say, laughing just a little while he moves more papers around.

"What can I do for you, Chase? I'm trying to get out of here on time for once. My son Ash is coming over for dinner and evidently has some news that can't be told over the phone," he says with that ever-present scowl.

"Just wanted to give an update from the assessment at Mac today, you know, since you sent me as some sort of punishment."

"Ha ha, believe me, going to that team was no punishment for you, and we both know it. Let me guess—you saw the new driver they have," Jasper smugly says, leaning back in his chair.

"Yeah, well, granted, that was a plus. You still could have given me a little heads-up. I'm sure that it wasn't just a last-minute thing; you just wanted to see if I could work on the fly. Well, joke's on you. It went swimmingly, and now I'm headed home to drink a beer and do nothing." *Wow, that sounded as pathetic as I am right now.*

"Really living that single life, aren't you, Bryant?" he says as he stands to leave.

"Listen, I sent you because you could work on the fly. You don't have to have a plan, and sometimes that's the best thing. Have a good night, Chase. I'll see you in the morning." And he's out the door before I can even get another word in.

I sit in his office for a little longer after Jasper leaves, replaying what he said just a few moments ago.

Well, damn, guess he actually does like me—that, or I just have the word "sucker" tattooed on my forehead.

WALKING into my house after grabbing dinner on the way home, I'm met at the door by the one person who will always be happy to see me when I come home. Miller is my two-year-old golden retriever. I couldn't even imagine being in this city without him.

Once I take Miller for his walk and get him settled for the night, I flip on the TV. Normally, I turn on the sports center or one of the other stations just so I can stay in the know of what's going on in the sports field, in case one of our local superstars is having some issues that might land them on our doorstep in the next few days. But it's all quiet on that front.

Just as I'm getting ready to turn the channel, that siren of a woman appears on the screen. Damn, I was so hyper-focused on thinking about Mila that I made her appear on the screen.

The reporter talks about the up-and-coming racers in the NASCAR world and ones to watch this season when they head down to Daytona in a few weeks. NASCAR Speedweeks and Mila Michelson are in the NASCAR community.

Son of a bitch, the woman just will not leave my head now. And, of course, the sadist that I am, I decide that googling her is the best idea in the world. Because why not? Not only is this a woman who I can't have because we work together occasionally, but she is so far out of my league it's unreal.

Mila Michelson is twenty-four years old, originally from California, currently living in North Carolina after getting picked up by one of the smaller teams to run the Busch series two years ago, and has slowly made a name for herself among the men in the sport. A few months ago, Mila signed with Mac Motorsports to be their third driver. Mila had been reportedly dating a baseball player with the Boston Revs, but that was short-lived as she moved to Charlotte and he was in Boston. Mila will be a full-time driver with Mac and is to compete for Rookie of the Year in the Cup Series starting in Daytona.

Ugh, what the hell is wrong with me? Get it together, Bryant. She's just any other woman.

This just goes to show that I need to get laid. That's all it is. I need to get her off my mind. I need to stop feeling like I'm in second place and take what I want. And I know just where to go to feel like that—the one place where no one knows me, and I can let my dominant side loose.

Walking up to the black door in downtown Charlotte a little less than an hour later, I'm on edge. The entire car ride, I couldn't just let it go. Nope, I had to replay every interaction we had today. Stepping out of my vehicle, I make my way across the street. If you glance up at the building, you would just assume that it's a normal area of town—maybe a restaurant or even a hotel for the elite—but looks can deceive; it's actually one of the premier BDSM clubs in the state of North Carolina, and I have a membership.

FOUR HOURS LATER, I lie sprawled out on the plush bed in one of the red rooms, stroking my sub's back as she sleeps beside me, completely drained from our fun. I thought once I punished Carolina for her brat behavior, some of my need would dissipate, but it only seemed to grow. She could tell that I was in a different head space tonight. She has been my sub the last few times I've come in, and she ticks all my boxes. Rolling to the edge of the bed and sitting up, I turn back to look at the beautiful woman lying fast asleep. Carolina is the type of woman I am drawn to. The brat in her called to my dominant side from the first time we met. But now that Mila has come into my world, she's all I can think about. Dark hair, chocolate-brown eyes, and curves in all the right places.

Standing up, I reach for the bottle of water on the end table and look around for my clothes. Time to head back to real life and figure my shit out. I can't keep coming here just to get my dominant side to calm down.

I make sure one last time that Carolina is content and knows I'm leaving before I close the door behind me and head toward my truck.

An hour later, I'm standing under the shower, still trying to come down from my high and wrap my head around the fact that I have to work not only with a woman who has already gotten under my skin but with the guy who took the girl who wasn't even mine to start with. This is going to be fun-freaking-tastic.

Chapter 7
Mila

You never know how much stress a person can endure until you're in the middle of the storm. And this press tour has definitely been my tornado. Who would have guessed being female and entering a male-dominated sport would be this much? Oh, wait, Grace warned me, but I just thought it was a crazy notion that people might just get on board and let me drive. I get people may want to take an interest in me and my skills, but it's not like I'm the first female driver to come through the cup series.

Taking a deep breath, I finish drying my hair and packing my thoughts away into the deep, dark place I keep them so that when I step out of my house, the only thing that the public sees is the bright and shiny driver that I need to be. Not the stressed-out version.

Deep breath, Mila. You can do this.

Stepping out onto the back porch, I breathe in the fresh air and just listen to the water and the birds. The one thing that I love the most about North Carolina is the beautiful scenery. Charlotte is close enough that you get the mountains in one direction and the beach in the other. Less than three hours in either direction, I can get whichever environment I need. I sip my coffee and sit down in one of the Adirondack chairs that Grace just insisted I needed for the porch, and take in the water, lightly smacking against the pier just down the way.

I'm so caught up in my head that I don't even hear Grace come up the steps until she literally scares the shit out of me.

"Earth to Mila, hello," Grace says, looking at me as if she's been standing there for more than just a few minutes.

"Shit, Grace, how long have you been there?" I say, looking up at her as I wipe the coffee that has sloshed on my leg.

"Wow, you are really in your own world this morning, Mila. What's going on with you?" Grace asks, looking at me like she's trying to answer her question.

"It's nothing, really; it's just been a long few days, and the media seems to have made me the world's one and only female racer. You know, just another day of the week."

Grace laughs as she comes to sit beside me. "You know, Mila, being in this sport is always fun. One day, the media wants to know every detail, and then the next, they couldn't care less. So you just have to ride the storm out."

"Well, Mrs. McCall, what's on the agenda today?" I laugh as I sip my coffee. Grace may act like a hard-ass to most people, but with me, I get to see the side that only a select few do.

"You're hilarious, Mila, and don't make me feel like an old married woman with the *Mrs.* on me." She rolls her eyes at me with a laugh of her own.

"And just so you know, today, your day is simple. Drive."

"Seriously, that's all I have today. Just driving?"

"Yep, that's it. You get to spend the entire day in the sim lab, and I get to spend the day with my husband," she says, wiggling her eyebrows.

Looking out over the lake, I can't help but smile. I get to drive all day. No media, no video calls. I get to do what I love.

"Come over for supper tonight. Matt's grilling out later with Ryan and Tinley. We would love you to join us."

Sounds like fun. I stand up from my chair and pour what little coffee I have left over the balcony. Time to head to the sim lab and just drive.

A FEW HOURS LATER, I'm setting up my spec for the first track that I need to focus on. Daytona is a monster, and it's where the world will see if I'm ready to play in the big sandbox. Once all the settings are ready, I sit down to practice.

Three hundred laps. That's how long I sit in the chair. Three hundred laps to get the track under me. Yes, I've run the actual track in person, but on the level that is expected of me with the best in the world, I need to make sure that I know just where to run and how to run it. Granted, the sim machine is never the same as the actual track, but it gives me a brief view of what it could be like. In one short month, we will be at Speedweek and then the Duels, and then, if all goes to plan, I'll be running in the "Great American Race."

Finishing up the day, I grab a bottle of water as I leave the sim room and slam into the hardest chest I have ever come in contact with.

"Wow, Michelson, where's the fire?" I hear the deep timbre of the one voice I can't get out of my head. Looking up, I'm met with the beautiful green eyes behind the dark-rimmed glasses of Chase.

"Mila, are you okay? You're staring," he says with a light laugh.

Clearing my throat, I take a step back from Chase. "Sorry about that. I was just heading out."

"It's fine. It's not every day a beautiful woman runs into you in the middle of a hallway," he says with a small smirk on his face.

"What are you doing here? I don't have another assessment, do I?"

"Nope, I'm just explaining the paperwork to the crew chiefs," he clarifies, "so that everyone is aware of the expectations, and we're all on the same page."

Looking down at the floor, I try to figure out what else I can say to continue the conversation, but nothing comes. I am a strong, confident woman, but when Chase is around, my brain goes stupid. What the hell is wrong with me? Why do I seem to be a different person around him?

"It was nice to see you again, Mila," he says with that small smirk again that makes me melt, then walks away with me standing in the hallway.

Pivoting on my heels, I head in the opposite direction, kicking myself for not talking to Chase more.

"So LET me get this straight: you bump into a hot-as-hell guy, lose your ability to speak, and now you're standing in my kitchen drinking tequila because you didn't know what to say. Did I get that all correct?" Grace says, looking at me like I've lost my damn mind while I take yet another shot.

"Whoa, what is going on here?" I hear Matt ask as I get yet another shot ready.

"If you must know, Matthew, I am a confident, know-what-I-want woman, and I deserve to get what I want. Yet today, I could not make my brain form a complete sentence. So I'm throwing myself a little pity party before I have to sit down to dinner with all you lovey-dovey couples. Now, if you walk away, I would like to talk with Grace," I say, giving him the side-eye before turning back around.

"Yep, I know when to walk away, but just for the record, that level of sass is nothing I haven't dealt with from this one, so you're gonna have to do better than that to get me to not ask questions," he says before grabbing the steaks from the fridge and walking back outside.

As I turn back toward Grace, I notice her eyes are fixed firmly on the back of Matt's ass as he walks outside. Ugh, why did I come tonight? I could have just stayed at home and had my pity party.

I hear the front door open, and Tinley's voice comes from the entry.

"In the kitchen, Tin. Mila is drinking herself into a stupor," she says with a laugh.

"Thanks," I say, throwing another shot back, wincing as the burn takes over.

"Ummm, okay, to what do I owe the day drinking?" Tinley asks and comes to stand beside me. I give Grace the side-eye as she tells her about my day.

"But the best part of the story I haven't even told you. Mila, why don't you tell Tinley who this man is?" Grace says with a huge smile on her face.

With my face in my hands, I look up at Grace.

"Chase Bryant."

And at that moment, you could hear a pin drop, just as Ryan comes around the corner with Matt.

Tinley looks at me like I have just burst into flames. *Umm, did I say something wrong? Are they related? What is going on?*

"Chase is the reason you lost your ability to speak and why you're day drinking?" Matt finally speaks up when the tension becomes so thick that you can cut it with a knife.

"Yep, he's the reason. Now, will someone please explain to me what is going on and why Tinley looks like someone kicked her puppy?"

Clearing her throat, Tinley finally speaks.

"Chase and I have a history of sorts. Long story short, I went on a blind date with Chase the same day I met Ryan. We hung out a few times while Ryan and I figured our shit out. Chase is a really great guy, sweet and smart, and was always a gentleman with me. So I don't want you to feel you can't be around him or even date him if you choose to." She moves to stand beside Ryan.

"Thanks for clueing me in. I had wondered what was up the other day when the air was very thick between Chase and Ryan when we did our assessments. So that makes so much sense now. But the only problem is we work together, so I can't cross that line even if I might want to scratch this itch. It's hard enough to be a female in the male-dominated world but to be the one who sleeps with someone on staff—it's a line I have to take a hard no on. Even if I want to."

Chapter 8
Chase

The last few weeks went by in a blur. Jasper seems to think it's fun to give all the new grumpy old men to me. But it kept me busy and my mind off that dark-haired siren.

"Chase, a word, please," Jasper says from his office as I'm passing by him with my second cup of coffee this morning.

"What's up, Jasper? And please tell me it's not that I'm getting yet another grump on my schedule today. It's like I'm the official magnet for them lately."

"Nope, not today. I know you have enough on your plate at the moment. I actually have some news. Mac Motorsports wants you to be their new therapist. In case anything happens, but heaven forbid that be the case," he says with a smug smile on his face.

"Um, thanks, I guess. But honestly, how much would a NASCAR driver really need from a sports medicine therapist?"

"Your task is to regularly communicate with the crew chief every week and ascertain the necessary preparations for the driver and crew prior to the race. They may need nothing, or they may need small treatments."

"Okay, sounds like a plan. I'll send the crew chiefs an email right now so that they have my email and cell phone number in case something comes up and I may not be in the clinic."

"Thanks for being flexible on this, Chase. I knew I chose the right person to oversee this client."

"No problem, sir," I say as I leave his office. Yeah, the right person, indeed. If only he knew the dilemma I was having right now with wanting to stay as far away from Ryan McKenzie as I can but be close to Mila Michelson. Taking a deep breath, I head toward my next patient.

FRIDAY MORNING, and I'm sitting at my desk typing up my notes on Mr. Donald's rehab when I feel a presence standing over me. I would know that smell anywhere. It's been a core memory since I laid eyes on her in the living room all those years ago. Pulling my glasses off, I look up to see Tinley standing in front of me.

"Hi, Chase, long time no see," she says as I move to stand.

"Tinley, wow, you look beautiful. Ummm, to what do I owe this pleasure? It's been a while."

Tinley looks around the clinic. "Can we go somewhere and talk?" she asks, glancing around at the patients now staring this way.

"Yeah, of course," I say, motioning her into the conference room.

"What's going on, Tin? I haven't talked to you in three years, and you just show up out of the blue? It's kind of freaking me out, if I'm being honest."

Tinley giggles just a little at my statement. "Listen, I know you saw Ryan a few weeks back when you came to the race shop. And I'm so sorry about the way things went down when we were in college. But I want you to know that Ryan is a good man, and I think if you give him a chance, you might actually see y'all are very similar."

"Hang on, Tin. Where is this coming from? I was nothing but

nice when I saw Ryan at the shop. I came in, did my job, and then went about my day."

"No, no, it's nothing like that. I just didn't want you to feel awkward when you had to go to the shop," she says, looking down at her feet, spinning the engagement ring on her finger.

Damn, she's still the same Tinley from college. Unsure of herself one minute and taking charge the next.

Tinley finally looks up at me, and I keep my eyes on her as she brings those blue eyes to mine. "I can promise you I am nothing but a professional with work. If Ryan has an issue, then he needs to come to me. Not send you here in his place. He can man up and talk to me."

"Ryan didn't send me." Her cheeks flush.

"Let's just say another driver might have mentioned you, and I didn't want it to be an issue with our history."

I stand there for a second, just staring at her. Huh, another driver, that dark-haired siren, was asking about me. Well, I'll be damned.

"Well, now that we agree, I think I'll leave you to your thoughts that have just come into your head," she says with a giggle and leaves me standing in the conference room.

Mila Michelson, you little minx, this day just got a little better. But the only issue is—she's a freaking client. Dammit.

SATURDAY AND SUNDAY are the only days when I have to do absolutely nothing. And that's what I intend to do this weekend. Mac Motorsports, along with the other teams, left for Daytona today for Speedweek, so I know my week will be just the normal physical therapy clients. I won't have to risk running into Mila at the shop and being tempted to touch that amazing body she has.

Tinley's words from Friday play over in my head: *"Let's just say another driver mentioned you..."* Ugh, get it together, Bryant. She's off-limits.

I lace up my shoes and grab Miller's leash. Might as well get some of this energy out, not just for me, but for Miller as well. The crazy weather we have been having has kept my poor boy cooped up in the house all week.

Popping my earbuds in and turning on the latest audiobook I have on my playlist, I start my run.

Four miles and five chapters later, I'm exhausted, and Miller just acts like he could go more.

Leaning down, I rub his head. "Sorry, bud, but I'm tapped out. Why don't we head back to the house?" He gives me sad eyes like I've just told him we can never come back outside, but he walks with me back toward the apartment.

When we get to the apartment, I pour him a bowl of water from the bottle I had and grab one for myself from the fridge, kicking my shoes off before heading to the shower.

I strip out of my sweaty clothes and throw them in the hamper beside the closet, just as my phone buzzes with an alert.

> Jasper: Wanna tell me who you pulled into the conference room yesterday?

I have to laugh at Mr. Nosy. I was wondering how long it might be before he called or texted. Hell, I expected him to grab me as soon as Tinley left. But he never did.

> Me: Just to get you off my back, that was Tinley Cash, well soon-to-be McKenzie. We had history in college until she picked Ryan over me, and she was just making sure it wasn't awkward for me to work together with him.

> Jasper: Shit, I did not know, man. I would have picked someone else had I known.

> Me: It's history, all's good, we moved on. End of story.

> Jasper: If you say so. I'm headed out to California this week with the family, so if you need me, just text or call.

> Me: Will do, y'all be safe and tell Ash I said hey and congrats.

A few weeks ago, Jasper got the news that his son had made it to the Blue Angels and that his first show was coming up soon.

After turning on the shower, I let the warm water run over me, standing under the spray. Gotta say, this week has been both trying and eye-opening in the same beat. Mila may not want to cross the line, but after what Tinley said, I can't help but wonder if, given the right incentive, she might just want to have a little fun.

THURSDAY FINALLY ARRIVES, and I'm sitting in front of the TV watching the Duels at Daytona. Ryan and Matt are in the first duel, and Mila is in the second.

The Duels are simple enough to keep up with two 150-mile qualifying races that determine the starting positions for the Daytona 500 from third to fortieth. The races are part of the Daytona 500 qualifying format. Each race comprises sixty laps around the 2.5-mile oval, so unless they qualify on the pole or second, race your way into the starting spot.

Never in my life have I ever been as invested in NASCAR as I am right now. Granted, I watched it growing up and knew about the sport, but having athletes' programs that I'm a part of brings a different level of interest.

When the green flag drops on the first duel, I take a deep breath and just watch.

Chapter 9
Mila

Duels at Daytona Day

Thursday morning, I wake up knowing that today, I will run my first official cup race. Later, it feels different from any other race day. I feel like my nerves are shot, and honestly, I might throw up at any moment. I knew I would be nervous, but I never expected this level.

As I'm stepping out of my bathroom in the race hauler, I hear a knock on the door. Opening it, I see Grace standing at the bottom step. "Whoa, Mila, you look like you're going to throw up at any second. What's going on?"

"Thanks, Grace, that's just what I needed to hear," I say, turning around and heading toward the fridge to grab a power drink.

Sitting down on the couch across from her, I let out a sigh. "I'm just a little nervous about racing later, okay? Is that what you want to hear?" I ask her, looking down at the bottle and pulling the label off as I have my internal freak-out.

"Mila, look at me. You are badass and ready to race these boys, and I would say even beat them. You need to channel that inner driver and show them how it's going to be. Don't go out there thinking you are anything but amazing. I know it's a lot of pressure to go out and be the woman in a man's world, but you also have to see that you deserve to be there."

Taking a deep breath, I let her words move through my mind and settle into my soul. I can do this. I've earned my spot, and I've worked for years to get here. I do not need to think of myself as not worthy; hell, I deserve it as much as anyone else.

Standing up, I shake off all the nerves that I had just let consume me and turn my music up.

"Okay, Grace, I'm gonna let you in on a little pre-race ritual that I have." She looks at me for a moment, trying to figure out what I have in store.

Grabbing her hand, I dance.

She laughs as she joins in. "So let me get this straight: you dance the nerves out?"

"Yep, when I'm anxious, I dance it out. Now come on, shake it."

After dancing with Grace, it's time to suit up and head to my car. Grace had left a little while ago to see Matt before his race. Two of my teammates got into the same duel, which left me alone. This can be a terrible deal at Daytona since drafting is such a big deal. But shit happens, and we adjust.

When I get to my car, I see Grace and Tinley approaching.

"Hey ladies, here to see me off?" I say, laughing at how close we have become over the last few months.

"We just wanted to make sure you know you have a support team behind you, and whatever you face, we face them together."

"Thanks, ladies. I couldn't have asked for a better family than the one that I am forming here."

"Now go out there and show this boys' club just what a badass you really are," Tinley says.

Nodding my head, I climb into my seat and strap in. The only thing standing between me and the Daytona 500 is sixty laps and twenty other drivers.

With the position I qualified for earlier this week, I'm starting in the middle of the pack, which can be great but also stressful. I need to be toward the front because Matt and Ryan finished in the top ten in their duel. But also, that's the more likely spot for a wreck when the race gets close to being completed. Talking with my crew chief, he wanted me to get a feel of the car and to race hard, but not at the level I would on Sunday. So, as the green drops, I'm trying to get the draft under control without taking out the entire back end of the field.

"Mila, I need you to settle down just a little. You don't need to push as hard as you are," I hear my crew chief say over the radio.

"I'm just making sure they know I'm here and that I'm not some little doll out here playing driver, is all."

"Well, you keep bumping Kyle like that, and you're going to learn really quick."

"Roger that." I back off just a little from Kyle's bumper.

Fifteen laps down out of sixty, and I'm getting the hang of the draft. But I do feel like a lone wolf out here.

"Any chance you can get me some help here?" I ask my spotter as we pass the finish line.

"On it, Mila," my spotter says.

Five laps later, and my spotter finally comes back on the line.

"Okay, if you can get to Ty, he's willing to ride with you to the front. He's been watching your numbers and sees you have a fast car."

"Great, tell him I'm coming." Dropping my car into the next gear, I set out to find Ty and attach to him.

Fifteen laps to go, and Ty and I went from the middle of the pack to the front. Both of our cars were fast, but when we got together, we took off. I never imagined I would run mid-pack at Daytona, let alone have the chance to be top five in the duels, but here I sit.

"Okay, Mila, now's the time. You can do this in one of two ways. We can slingshot around him coming out of turn four, or you can play it safe and stick with him and be runner-up. It's your call, but I need to know which option so I can calm my nerves," my crew chief says, laughing in the headset.

"Alright, boss, I'm going for it."

I've never been a girl to back down from a challenge, and that is damn sure not going to start today with the second-row spot in the Daytona 500 on the line.

As we make our way around turns three and four, I push Ty just a little more aggressively, letting him know that, hey, I may pull out from behind you.

Just as I'm dropping down, I'm hit in the right back bumper, sending me forward and turning Ty into the car next to him. As I try to get my car to straighten up, I'm pushed hard into the grass, and with the rain from earlier in the week, I'm unable to slow down. All I can do is try not to get hit head-on by turning the car. Just as I'm slowing, I slam into the wall.

Opening my eyes to get my bearings, I realize I am no longer in the car but in a hospital bed. As I slowly look around, I see Grace sitting beside me with a worried look on her face and her phone in her hand, typing a million miles a minute.

"Grace, what happened?" I say so quietly I don't think she hears me as she keeps looking at her phone.

"Grace." I try to talk a little louder, and that gets her to look up.

"Oh, Mila, you're awake. Thank God," she says, concern written all over her face.

When she passes me some water, I take a small sip and lay my head back on the pillow.

"Grace, what happened? Why am I in the hospital?" I ask, wanting her to be my friend right now and not my PR person.

"Let me get the doctor, Mila. He can tell you better than me," she says, rushing out of the room to find the doctor.

I try to sit up, but it feels like my entire body experienced the sensation of being run over. What the hell happened? The last thing I remember is being hit and spinning toward the grass. It shouldn't have been that bad of a crash. I have hit the wall that same way a million times and never found myself in the hospital.

Grace walks back into the room with Matt trailing behind her and an older-looking version of Dr. McSteamy. Damn, these must be some wonderful drugs.

"Hello, Mila, I'm Dr. Thomas, the orthopedic surgeon who stabilized your leg and ankle when you came in yesterday."

What the hell? I've been out of it for a whole day, and did he just say he stabilized my leg and ankle? That can't be right. I don't feel like I have something broken.

"Mila, did you hear Dr. Thomas?" Grace asks, looking at me with so much concern.

"I'm sorry, Dr. Thomas. Did you tell me I have a broken leg and ankle?" I ask, clearing my throat a little more.

"I did, Mila. I'm sorry to say that you have a pretty serious break, and you may require additional surgeries if the bones don't set the way they need. As soon as you are stable, we will fly you back to Charlotte, and you can meet with the team there and start a treatment plan."

Additional surgery—that means that I'm out for most of the race season. I can't be out. I just started. On the brink of making the Daytona 500, on the brink of proving to all those little girls that they can compete with the boys without fear. Now what am I supposed to do? Sit on the couch and watch each week?

"Mila, I'm so sorry. I'll let you rest and have the nurses come give you some more pain meds so that you can sleep off the anesthesia a little more before we get the paperwork ready to transport you," he says before leaving the room.

I just lie there staring at the ceiling, wondering what the hell I am going to do now.

"Mila, what can I get you?" I hear Grace ask.

Shutting down is the only thing I feel like doing right now.

"Grace, can you and Matt just... I just want to be alone."

"Mila, you can't shut us out. You need your friends around you. We are your family. You said that yourself before—"

I cut her off before she can even say the word... *race*.

"Grace, I want to be alone now. Please leave." I use a voice I'm not sure many people use with Grace McCall, but I need her to know that I don't want people around, even if they are turning into my family.

"Come on, Red, let's leave Mila to her thoughts." Matt leads her out the door, turning around to look back at me before nodding and closing the door. I know he gets it. He's a driver, and I'm sure if anyone can tell her how I'm feeling right now, it's him.

As soon as the door clicks shut, I let the first tear fall.

Chapter 10
Chase

I sat in shock. I've watched Mila's wreck play on repeat for the last half hour—her car slamming into the wall, and the crew running to her and pulling her out as the car catches fire. Her lying on the ground, talking to the EMS crew. Then being loaded into the ambulance and taken away.

That was over four hours ago now, and still no update. Why hasn't Grace sent anything out? I think about reaching out to Tinley to check on her but then think better of it. It's not my place. I'm not anything to Mila. Hell, I don't even know her outside of the brief interaction that we had the two times we have even seen one another. As if thinking about her brought up the update, my phone pings with an alert that I had set on it for the drivers, just in case I didn't have the news or race coverage on.

Press Release:

From Mac Motorsports

Today, during the Duel Race at Daytona, rookie sensation Mila Michelson was involved in a very serious crash. Mila received treatment from the best trauma doctors in the state at the local hospital. Once she was stabilized, the doctors transported her to surgery to repair her broken leg and ankle.
It is with great sadness that Mila will be out for the majority of the season because of this wreck. We wish her a speedy recovery, and she will be trans-

ported back to Charlotte within the next few days to possibly have another surgery on her ankle before starting her rehab in the coming weeks.

Please keep Mila in your thoughts and prayers as she heals and gets back to racing as soon as she can.

Just as I finish reading the release, my phone rings. Seeing Jasper's name on the screen, I answer, even though I would rather not talk to anyone at the moment.

"Chase, I just saw the press release on Mila. Do we know anything?" I hear the concern in his voice. He's been in the field long enough to know that when they say leg and ankle, that recovery is not the easiest, and it's gonna be hell on her.

"No, not yet. I just got the same release as you. I'm just waiting to hear from Grace about what will need to be done when they return to Charlotte. From reading the release, she may have to have another surgery, so I guess things are up in the air until then."

"Well, keep me in the loop if you hear anything before I get back into town. If not, I'll see you in the office on Monday," he says before hanging up the phone.

I stare at the release and reread the caption three more times before setting my phone down on the table and standing up. Pacing the room, I'm trying to figure out what needs to be done for Mila and the treatment plan to get her back in the car and doing what she loves the fastest. As if Miller can sense my anxiety, he comes over to where I'm pacing and nudges me with his nose, just to make sure that I know he's with me, and it's going to be okay.

"Hey, bud. Yeah, it's gonna be okay. I'll figure out how to help that beautiful woman and put her back together."

Four days—that's how long it takes. Four long days of waiting after the Duels at Daytona and Mila's accident to finally hear from Grace on the next steps for Mila's recovery.

> Unknown: Hey. Tinley gave me your number. This is Grace btw.
>
> Me: Hey, Grace, that's fine. I've honestly been waiting for your call or text.

A few minutes later, my phone rings with Grace's name coming up.

"Hey, Chase, I just wanted to check in and give you an update on Mila since your clinic has been helping with the medicine side."

Grace tells me exactly what happened and what needs to be done now. Looking at the crash and then reading the release told little.

"I could have called Tinley, but I didn't want to overstep until I got confirmation from you about what actually happened."

"Sure, so when Mila hit the wall, she broke her tibia and fibula, along with her ankle bone. She's had one surgery so far to fix her leg bones but may need another once we all get back to Charlotte tomorrow and the ortho guys check her out. But we won't know for certain until that appointment," Grace tells me.

Taking a deep breath, I am relieved to hear that it wasn't her entire leg shattered and just the lower bones. That means that the rehab is still going to be rough, but not anything I'm sure she can't handle. "Six weeks to get her back to racing again."

"As soon as I get more information tomorrow, I'll call you, and we can set you up and help with rehab. Thanks again for answering my call, Chase. I know this may be a weird situation, but I know that she's going to need a support system and, well, small worlds and all." She says this with a small laugh before hanging up.

Hanging up the phone, I push back from my desk and just stare at the wall for what feels like an eternity. A knock at the door gets my attention as Jasper comes into view.

"Hey, Jasper," I say, turning my chair back around to focus on the papers I was looking over before Grace called.

"Give me the rundown, Chase. I heard the tail end of the conversation as I was walking down the hall." He comes to sit down across from me.

"She's got ORIF (open reduction internal fixation of the tibia and fibula) and also a broken ankle. Tomorrow, they will fly home and have a meeting with the ortho guys here. After that, they will determine if additional surgery is necessary or if the ankle can heal from being in the cast. Grace is going to give me an update after that appointment tomorrow, and then we'll know when rehab can begin."

"Damn, that's a rough break. One bone is tough, but both—that's going to be a process," Jasper says, rubbing his hand through his hair.

"Yeah, it is, but she'll be okay. She has to. Racing is the only thing she wants to do, so as long as that drive is there, she can do it."

Jasper goes to stand, knocking his knuckles on the desk as he leaves. "Just be careful, Chase. She's going to be one of two ways when she comes back home. Angry as hell or a shell of a person because of it. Keep your head on straight, and help her with the rehab. And you know the rule—we don't get involved with our patients."

I sit at my desk looking at my paperwork for what feels like forever, replaying Jasper's comments over in my head. Don't get involved. Until this moment, I hadn't even thought of getting involved with Mila. We work together, and she's gone more often than she's home. She's off-limits. I know this.

GRACE HAD CALLED on Friday to let me know that they had gotten home, and Mila was resting. Luckily, they didn't need to do another surgery at the moment on her ankle. The doctors want to let her leg heal, and the ankle is the least of the issues at the moment. So they had her put in a cast from thigh to toe, and they think the ankle may heal from that alone.

After work, I stop by the bar on the way home. It has been a week, and I just need a little time to think.

"What can I get you, bud?" the bartender asks as I sit down.

"Scotch neat, please," I say, looking around the bar. He comes back a few minutes later, placing the drink in front of me.

I mumble thanks to him as I down the shot. "Can I get another one?"

"Sure, bud, been that kind of week, huh?"

"You have no idea," I tell him.

When he places the second one in front of me, I take my time with it, watching the other customers come and go. My mind is a million miles away when a familiar scent gets my attention. Tinley. I would recognize that scent anywhere.

"Hey, stranger, drinking alone?" she asks.

Looking over my shoulder, I'm hit with those gorgeous blue eyes. I shake my head and just stare at her for a moment.

"What brings you to my bar, Tin?" I say with a smile.

"Just came from seeing Mila and needed a drink. Ryan and Matt are parking the truck, so Grace and I wanted to come on in. I saw you sitting over here as she was getting to our table and wanted to say hello. You looked like you were in your head just now," she says with such sweetness.

Yeah, it's definitely been one of those weeks. Patient overload and then trying to figure out how we can help Mila when she starts rehab has me stressed to the max. But I don't tell her that.

"It's nothing, just the normal work week."

"Well, you're welcome to join us for drinks if you'd like. I know Grace would love to see you, especially since you're going to be helping Mila."

"Nah, y'all have your night." I finish my scotch, putting a fifty on the bar, before I stand and pull her into a quick hug.

"Have a good night, Tin. I'm sure I'll be seeing you around."

Walking toward the door, I see Ryan standing over by the table with Matt and give him a small nod before I leave.

Chapter 11
Mila

"Grace, you have got to let me get out of this bed. I'm going fucking crazy."

"Nope, the doctor said you are to stay in bed another two days, and I intend to make sure that happens come hell or high water. Now sit your ass down and stop testing me."

I blow out a frustrated breath. "Jeez, Mom, okay. I'll stay in bed. Damn." With a huff, I lie back down. Since coming back from Daytona, I have just moved from one bed to the next. It's been beyond boring, and there are only so many books a person can read on their e-reader until it starts to feel the same.

Am I bitter right now? Yep. Am I pissed I can't race for the next six weeks at the minimum? Yep. But the thing that has me in the worst mood at this second is that I can't get out of the damn bed.

"Tomorrow starts your therapy, so you need to rest because I'm sure you're going to be exhausted when that begins."

"Grace, you don't have to stay with me and take me places. I can call my mom and have her stay with me while I have to go to all these appointments."

As soon as we got back to North Carolina, my mom flew in from California and stayed a few days to make sure I was settled. However, being a teacher, she had to get back home, and I understood. I didn't need her here. I love my mom, but the woman is a helicopter. Between my bad mood and her being everywhere I turned, I was glad she left. But that also left me with no options to get to and from appointments. Enter Grace.

Grace moved me into her guest room and told Matt in no uncertain words that I was staying, and that was that. So here I sit, a houseguest who can't get out of bed except to go to the bathroom. And there's a freaking wheelchair beside the bed for when I want to leave the room. I can't put any weight on my leg for four weeks, and then we will assess if my ankle needs to be repaired after that.

One more day, Mila, then you start rehab.

Looking down at my leg, I curse at myself.

How stupid, Mila. You were two laps away from being in the Daytona 500, and you couldn't just ride behind Ty and take the spot. Nope, you had to try for the win. Now you're broken, and it's all your fault. You literally have no one to blame but yourself.

Letting out a sigh, I feel the tears form, and I can't help but get even more mad at myself.

Stupid girl, don't let your emotions get the better of you.

"You want to be the best, then you earn it. Don't be weak in front of the other competitors or the media. Show them you're supposed to be here." I hear my dad's voice echoing in my head.

A knock on my door has me stilling my face. "Come in."

"Hey, Mila," Tinley says.

Over the last week, I've gotten to know Tinley a little better. That girl is good as gold and will do anything for you if you're a part of her circle.

Taking a breath, I shift on the bed, trying to get a little comfortable, but the damn cast makes it hard to even adjust somewhat without my leg screaming in pain.

"Mila, don't move. I just came by to check in and see if you need anything. I'm headed to the track with Ryan and Matt but wanted to make sure that Nurse Grace has everything she needs while we are gone. And also make sure y'all have food because we all know Grace isn't the best cook." She says this with a laugh.

"I heard that, you heifer," Grace says, coming into the bedroom. "And I'll have you know that Cowboy has taught me a few things."

"Outside the kitchen doesn't count, darling," Tinley tells her before coming to stand close to me.

"Mila, I'll see you on Monday when we get back. Keep Grace in line, and I hope your first rehab goes okay tomorrow. Chase just might be the perfect guy to help with your treatment."

"Thanks, Tinley."

Chase—that's who gets to help. Of course, that's who it would be. The guy who I can't make complete sentences with. The only problem is now he's going to see just how weak I am because of something that didn't have to happen.

I close my eyes to wrap my head around what is now my life.

Racing is all I have ever known. How can I just sit back and watch it continue around me? But I guess that's life. Shit, things happen, and you either roll with it or you let it drag you down. But at this moment right now, I'm not rolling with it, and I'm okay with that.

Trying to get settled, I drift off to sleep. When I wake a few hours later, I'm covered in sweat, and my heart is racing so fast I think it may come out of my chest.

The dream has been the same for the last few days. I'm right back in that car. Except now I'm the passenger, not the driver, and I'm telling the driver what is going on and what's about to happen. We slam into the wall, and I'm outside the car, watching the scene after the crash. I'm screaming as the EMTs pull me out of the car, and I notice that my leg is broken. Then it's the ride to the hospital and waking up to Matt and Grace telling me what happened.

It's like my life has turned into Groundhog Day, and my brain wants me to know what happened.

Trying to sit up is a bitch, but I am going to do it on my own. Grace has been beyond great, but it's the middle of the night, and I honestly just don't want to wake her to help me go to the bathroom. At some point, I've got to do things for myself, no matter how much it may hurt.

So I reach for my wheelchair, since I can't bear weight for a few weeks, and try to slide into it. And when I say slide, it's more of a roll. My leg is in a cast, and the drugs that I've been taking for the pain make my entire body feel like lead. But I sit in the chair without falling on my face.

Challenge one down. Now to make it to the bathroom before I pee all over myself. Wheeling over to the door, I soon see that the chair will not fit through the doorway, so I'm going to have to hobble over to the toilet. Shit, this just got harder. Ugh, I really don't want to get Grace out of bed for this. My pride is still too intact for that. Pulling myself to stand, I wobble just a little before I catch myself on the counter. Thank God this bathroom isn't huge. Okay, just a little farther, and I'll be there. Just as I go to move, my good knee gives out, and I hit the floor, taking the towel rack with me.

I'm lying on the bathroom floor when I hear Grace yell my name from the bedroom door.

"I'm in the bathroom, Grace," I say back, closing my eyes and trying like hell not to break down in front of her but failing miserably.

"Mila, what the hell are you doing?" I hear her say just as she comes into the bathroom.

"Oh, honey." Her voice has a little more sympathy as she sees me crying on the floor.

"I just wanted to go to the bathroom alone. It's the middle of the night, and I'm not three years old. I should be able to get up and do something. But look at me; I can't even stand long enough to do that." Anger rises the longer she looks at me.

"Mila, you just had surgery a week ago. Your leg is in a cast, and you're still recovering. It's okay to ask for help. Even if it's in the middle of the night," she replies as she helps me to sit up.

I rest my back against the cabinets, closing my eyes while I get my emotions back in check.

"I know this isn't the season you wanted, but you're going to be back to racing before you know it. Now, how about I help you, and then we can both get a little rest before your therapy starts tomorrow? Think you can humor me on that one time?" she asks.

Yeah, just once. Even though I know, deep down, it's going to be a lot more than once. Hell, I can't even stand on my own. How the hell can I get a bath without help? Guess I better get used to Grace seeing me like this.

"Bet you never thought going into PR that you might be your client's nurse at some point, did you?" I say, trying to lighten my mood.

Laughing, she says, "Yeah, out of all the things I do for you, this is the one that I didn't think I would have to do. But Mila, I want you to know you're one of my best friends, and I want you to ask for help. Even if it's something simple. You're not alone. We are family now."

After using the bathroom, with a little help from Grace, she gets me back in bed, and my body is screaming in pain. Taking a few pain meds, I drift off to sleep. Luckily for me, this time, the nightmares stay at bay, and I get a few hours of sleep.

The next morning, during the ride over to the physical therapy office, I'm a ball of nerves. It may be because of the unknown of what's to come and the plan, or maybe knowing I was going to see him.

Grace stops the car as close to the door as she can and waits for the nurse to come out and help me into the wheelchair before she leaves to park the car.

After getting all the paperwork in order and meeting some of the staff, I'm finally led back to the treatment area. Or, as I like to call it, hell on earth.

I'm sulking in my chair when I see Chase come walking over.

I have seen little of him yet since one of the other guys said he was finishing up with a patient and that he would meet us when he was done. Watching him now, with his scrubs on and those Clark Kent glasses and dark-blond hair just a little in his face, I have to smirk at the sight. He's the complete opposite of the guys who I normally find attractive, and there is something about him I can't put my finger on yet, but the way he carries himself is hot.

"Well, ladies, sorry to keep you waiting." His deep timbre of a voice breaks through my thoughts as I look up at him.

"Hey, Chase, busy morning, I see," Grace says, giving him a small hug.

"Yeah, we have a lot of knee replacements at the moment. It must be that season. How are you, Mila?" he asks, looking at me.

Let's see, how am I? Well, honestly, I'm in a shit mood if we are being honest. But I don't say that.

"I'm okay," is what I actually say.

"Yeah, I get that. I saw your X-rays, and that's a nasty break you have. But with the treatment plan I have set up, we should have you back to racing in no time," he says as sweetly as he can, trying to make my mood a little better.

"Not really sure what I can do at the moment, doc. This cast makes it impossible to stand up, let alone do anything else."

"Well, stick with me, and you will do more than you ever thought you could," he says with a smirk.

Damn him and that smile.

"Chase, I've got a few things to do at the office, and then I'll be back in two hours to pick Mila up," Grace says.

"Yeah, we may finish before that, depending on Mila's pain tolerance."

"I can take pain, Chase." My tone gets sharper the more they talk as if I'm not here.

"We'll see about that," he responds, his arms crossed as he finishes talking to Grace.

Chapter 12
Chase

Mila's mood has gone from bad to worse the longer our rehab session has gone on.

I understand she believes she has been dealt a bad hand, but things could have been much worse.

"You know that the longer you sit over there stewing on something, the longer this is going to take, right?" I learn really quickly that Mila does things on her own time—not when she's asked. It's like she's trying to test me. Guess I'm going to have to bring my dominant side out to play with her brat side that I'm coming to see.

"Chase, I refuse to jump when you say so. Unless you think that this benefits me in that race car, I will not do it," she sasses.

"Mila, for the love of God. All you have to do is lie on the table and roll your hips. It's not like I am asking you to run on your broken leg. Hell, I'm not even asking you to stand up. You're not allowed to do that for another two weeks. And that's only if I think you're ready. So if you want to follow my instructions and get out of that damn cast sooner, you will lie down on that table and do the hip exercise."

I let her sit for two more minutes before I am literally pulling her onto the table. I had moved us into a private room before we started so that if it got too tough and she needed to break, she could take one without the other patients staring at her. But now

I'm thinking this might not have been the best idea the moment I lay her down on the table.

"Do I have your attention now, Mila?" I say in a deeper voice, trying to get her to submit to me.

Those deep-brown eyes go wide for a moment, and her lush pink lips open and close for a beat before she finally clears her throat. But no words come out, only a head nod.

"I need your words, driver."

"Yes, sir," she says.

Letting her hips go, I stand back. Shit, what the hell am I thinking? I can't put my hands on her like that again. And I sure as shit can't have her calling me sir.

Taking another step back, I run my hand through my hair to get my mind back on the job at hand and not on all the ways I could have her on this exam table right now.

There's a knock at the door as I'm getting my shit together. Turning to see who it is, I pull the door open to find Jasper standing in front of me.

"Hey, Chase, just coming to see how the first day is going with Mila."

"Oh, we are just having the best time ever, Jasper," Mila says, sarcasm coming off in waves.

Jasper laughs as I turn around to glare at Mila.

"Got a bit of a spitfire in that one, don't ya, son?" Jasper says, clapping me on the shoulder.

"You do not even know," I grumble.

"I'll let you get back to it."

"Yeah, thanks, man."

Blowing out a breath, I head back over to the table to once again get Mila to fall in line with the exercise I want her to do.

"Mila, all I need you to do is slowly roll back and forth onto the table. This will help loosen your hip joints and will make it easier for you to get up and down. That cast is heavy as hell since it's almost your entire leg, and your hips are taking the extra impact."

Finally, she nods in acceptance and does the exercise I've instructed, but I can see in an instant that she's in pain.

"Mila, what hurts?" I ask, trying to adjust the movement for what she needs.

"Nothing, I'm fine. I can do it." Her teeth are clenched so tight that I think she may break one off.

"Yeah, that's a lie, and you know it. Now tell me what's hurting when you do that."

"I said I'm fine."

I step toward her once again. The smell of lavender instantly hits me when I stand at her injured leg, placing my hand on it to stop her movement.

Looking over at me, she finally stops, and when my eyes make contact, she has the start of tears.

"Shit, Mila. If this is too much, tell me. I can't help you if you don't talk."

"Chase, I'm really fine. That movement isn't what the problem is," she says, looking at the ceiling and wiping the tear that has fallen on her beautiful face.

Walking over to her, I pull her up into the sitting position.

She stares at me yet again with those brown eyes that are now a little red from the tears that want to escape, but she won't let them.

"I don't want to be a weak person, Chase," she says but then stops herself.

Grabbing a chair, I go to sit beside her. Being in physical therapy, you also have to listen to your patients. They go through a lot in a short amount of time. That's one thing people don't get. The amount of trauma people have to process when they rehab can be as much of a battle as they have when fixing a bone that was broken.

"Mila, being weak sometimes isn't a bad thing. It just means that you are processing."

"Chase, when people look at me, what do you think they see?" she asks, but I'm not sure if she wants an actual answer or if she just has a thought, so I wait and see if she continues.

"When they look at me, they see a pretty face. They don't see a race car driver or someone who has worked their ass off to get to the level I'm at. Nope, they see the dark hair and boobs and say, 'Yeah, she's the girlfriend.' Wrecking at Daytona just showed those people that I wasn't ready. They couldn't have cared less that I ran at the top all day. Nope, I wrecked, and that's what they took away from that race."

"Mila, those people are not who you race for. The ones who actually want you to succeed are those who you race for."

She wipes a few tears away as I hear the door to the treatment room open again. This time, Grace enters.

I turn around to see Grace's concerned face and stand.

Walking over to Grace, I put my hand on her shoulder, trying to tell her without telling her she's had a rough day.

"Mila, I'll see you in a few days for your next session. At home, I want you to work on the hip exercises." And I close the door behind me.

Chapter 13
Mila

Grace comes over to where I'm lying on the treatment table. Tears still silently fall from my eyes. I'm pissed and embarrassed at myself for crying. I didn't expect to open up to Chase about how I was feeling in that moment until it was out of my mouth before I could stop it.

"Hey, are you ready to head home?" Grace asks, coming to help me sit up on the table.

"Yeah, I've had all I can take for today."

Helping me to the wheelchair, Grace makes sure my leg is up, and then we head toward the car and home. Well, not my home, of course, because I can't do a fucking thing myself.

Ugh, this is going to be a long few weeks.

After stopping to grab supper at the local sushi bar, I'm finally sitting down with my leg propped up on so many pillows I can barely see over it when Grace finally talks.

"You know you don't have to be so tough all the time. It's okay to let people in."

"And by people, do you mean you and me, or are you talking about a certain dark-blond-haired Clark Kent?" I ask, looking over at Grace as she sets her wine down, facing me on the couch.

"Listen, I get that you're mad and that life seems like it's in the toilet right now, but I can promise you it's really not. So you had a setback. That doesn't mean you won't be back in no time."

Resting my head back on the couch, I look at the ceiling, just listening to Grace. I get it; I really do. My body is broken, but honestly, that's not the only thing. My spirit and drive also don't want to get on board with healing at the moment, and I'm okay with that. I want to be bitter, and I want to be mad. Hell, if I could, I would break a few objects, but I'm not too sure Grace or Matt would like that. So I'll just stick to being difficult.

"Mila, look at me."

"Listen, I've talked to all your sponsors, and they all agree that having you as their driver for the rest of the season is what they want. They want to see you come back from this stronger and better than when you got hurt. They are sticking it out. So we will get you through therapy, and then once we get the okay, we will start practicing in the car here in Charlotte. That way, as soon as they say yes, you're back in your car and pushing to win that first cup race."

I blink a few times, taking in what Grace said. The sponsors still want me. They don't think I'm just some driver who got hurt and now is looking for another place to land. It's that information that makes me want to try harder to get out of this cast and back into a car.

"Grace, thank you so much for everything you have and are doing. You may not know it, but you're kind of exceptional. And I'm lucky that you're not only a part of my team but also my friend."

"I wouldn't have it any other way, and I truly mean that. You're kind of exceptional yourself, Mila."

A FEW DAYS LATER, it's time to endure Chase's special brand of torture. Honestly, after the first day, I kind of got the impression that Chase was trying to break me or trying to turn me on. And he for sure turned me on more than broke me, even with my little crying fit I had.

"Well, if it isn't my favorite patient," Chase says as he cleans off the treatment table.

"For some reason, I think you may say that to all your patients, Chase."

"You could be right," I hear Jasper say as he passes by my treatment room.

"Chase Bryant, what kind of enjoyment am I in for today?"

"I thought we might see how that range of motion is going with your hip to start with. And if you don't give me too much lip, I might let you try to get in some arm weights. Since it's going to be a few weeks before we can work on putting weight on the leg, you need to keep your arm strength up."

Rolling my eyes, I wheel myself over to the table and wait for him to come and help me onto it. It's not like I could jump on the table with one leg.

After I lie down and Chase checks to make sure I will not roll off, he has me do a few reps of the hip flexors, and I'm surprised when he has no smart comeback when I do what I'm asked.

I sit up on the table after finishing the last set and notice Chase typing some notes into his tablet. Straining my neck to see what he's typing, I nearly fall off the table, but of course, before I face-plant, his muscular arms are around me, pulling me back up.

"Mila, what the hell are you doing?" he asks, looking at me with what I can only explain as fury.

Pulling back from him, I'm ready to go into defense mode.

"Well, Chase, if you must know, I was trying to see what you were typing about me."

Letting out a slow breath, he pushes his glasses onto the top of his head and comes to sit beside me. When he gets close enough, I can smell the amazing scents that are just so Chase.

"Okay, nosy, if you must know, I was emailing your crew chief. You see, I have to report each time you're here with the team so they know how you're doing and if any issues have come up. You know, since you're under my care and all."

Taking the tablet from him, I see the email to my crew chief he was finishing.

I hand it back to him and try to stand from the table to get into my wheelchair. But it's useless. He's right there, grabbing my hand and helping me to sit.

Every time this man touches me, my body wants more. My head and heart are in two different spaces about it though.

My heart says red alert; you can't fall for him. He may be great on paper, but you can't fall because you'll want to jump full force into a relationship. You don't do it easy anymore. You're not that girl. The next relationship is for the long haul.

Meanwhile, my head is screaming to just give in. Hell, just give him one night. Scratch the itch. He may be perfect for right now. Who says he even wants a relationship, anyway? You really don't know him.

Then I look down at my broken body and scream to myself for even thinking about him at all.

"Hey, you okay?" he asks, pulling my attention from my crazy thoughts. "You kind of zoned out just now."

"Yeah, I'm fine. Hey, thanks for today. Same time on Thursday?" I ask as I leave.

"Where are you going, Mila? You still have an hour left," he says with a small laugh.

"What? We aren't done?" My voice comes out a little softer than normal.

"Nope, not even close, sweetheart." He smirks at me as he pushes the wheelchair out to the main treatment area.

"I told you that if you showed me you could follow the instructions I gave you, you would be rewarded with the opportunity to do some strength training."

I'm sure I look like a freaking fish right now. But every time he uses a certain voice, I can't talk or think. Does he even know he is doing it?

Stumbling over my words, I finally get out, "Okay."

Chapter 14
Chase

Handing Mila the five-pound weights, I just take in the woman who is taking up so much time in my thoughts. The more time she's here, the more I want to take her therapy as slowly as possible just so I have more time with her. I know I can't do that, but hell do I want to.

Clearing my throat, I give her instructions on the weights to make sure that she doesn't move too much in the chair. It's about using her arms and shoulders only.

Rolling her eyes, she lifts the weights above her head and counts.

After doing the exercise for three counts of fifteen, I can tell she's on the verge of giving me sass because her huffs are getting more and more the longer she goes.

"You know I can lift over five pounds, right?" she says, handing me over the weights.

"Yeah, I know you can, but you see, it's not about the weights —it's about the motion, and you can't seem to get the motion to my liking."

"You have got to be kidding me right now. I literally just did a fuck ton, and you never once told me it was wrong," she says, her face turning a deep shade of red.

I bend down so I'm at eye level with her. "Mila, I couldn't care less how many you do. This brief assignment was to see if you would follow my instruction."

I step just close enough so only she can hear me. "And you drivers are so stubborn that you can't even tell when you don't follow the way I've told you," I say and step back from her.

"We're done for the day, Mila. See you in a few days."

"Hey, Grace, y'all have a nice day," I say before walking toward my office and getting as far away from that siren as I can before I do something that I can't control.

I'm sitting at my desk for a few hours trying to finish up paperwork when Jasper makes yet another appearance. I swear I haven't talked this much to him since he hired me. He never checks in on any of my other patients like he does Mila.

"You look like shit, man. Rough day with the driver?" Jasper asks, coming to sit in front of me.

I am wound so tight I don't have time for his shit, and my patience meter ran out about an hour ago.

Putting my glasses on the desk, I look up at Jasper.

"Is there something I can help you with, or have you just come in here to bust my balls about Mila?"

Laughing, he just shrugs. "Just checking in is all. Damn, she really has you in a tailspin, Chase."

Blowing out a breath, I glare at him.

"Have you ever had a woman drive you crazy, and yet you want to protect her all in the same heartbeat?"

"Yep, sure have," he says.

"Wanna clue me in on how to fix it?"

"Nope, because you're not ready for that answer just yet, son. You're going to have to go through it, and then I might give you that little bit of advice," he adds as he stands and heads for the door.

"But I will give you one thing. If you think she's worth all the trouble, then it will come easy. You won't have to work hard. But also, if she's worth it, then it can wait until she's no longer a client."

Well, shit, therein lies the problem. She's always going to be a client as long as she is with Mac Motorsports. And I will not make her choose. I would never do that.

Jasper closes the door as he leaves, and I'm left with my thoughts and the image of Mila. The girl has my head in a vise. One minute, she wants to submit to me, and the next, she's being a brat. The combination has me hard as a rock in seconds. Dammit, I can't be thinking of her.

Shaking my thoughts out, I grab my keys and laptop and head out for the night.

When I make it back to my apartment, Miller is waiting for me at the door. "Hey, bud, were you good today?" I ask like I'm going to get a response.

He jumps up and down, letting me know he's ready to go out for the night. I could use a run to clear my head, so I grab his leash and head out to run the dark-haired beauty out of my system before I do something stupid like text her. But hell, I would have to have her number for that.

During the run, all I could think of was texting Grace to get Mila's number. I picked up my phone more times than I like to admit, but I didn't hit send.

Miller whines when we get back to the apartment building. I know he loves being outside, but it's after nine at night, and I'm ready to shower and go to bed.

"Sorry, but time to go inside. I promise this weekend we will go to the park, and you can play, but it's dark, and it's time to go to bed."

He drops his head and follows me like the noble dog he is.

After getting him settled and eating just a little, I head to bed, but I just can't shake the desire to text Mila. I know I shouldn't cross the line, but she's in my head too much, and texting is safe, or so I think. So I hit send.

> ME: Hey, it's Chase. Could you give me Mila's number?

I stare at my phone for a few minutes, but when Grace doesn't reply, I think she may be asleep, so I decide to jump in the shower to wash the day off.

When I finish drying and wrap the towel around my waist, I notice I have a reply from Grace.

> Grace: And just what do you need her phone number for, Chase? (Smirking emoji)

Thinking to myself, I need to make it sound like it's for her treatment, not that I just want to have a reason to talk to her.

(Text bubbles)

> Grace: Trying to come up with a reason, aren't you, Chase? (Laughing emoji)

Damnit, Grace is like a human lie detector, even over text. Blowing out a breath, I text back.

> ME: Fine, yes, I want it for treatment stuff, but maybe I just want it as well.

> Grace: Yep, figured it out. I've been waiting for you to ask. Honestly, I can't believe you just didn't get it off the paperwork.

Smacking myself on the forehead, I had completely forgotten that her number would be on the forms she had to fill out when she started rehab. Wow, I really am an idiot. I can't even think of Mila. Now I have let Grace in on the fact that I want to talk to Mila outside of the office.

> ME: I'm trying to be professional here, Grace.

> Grace: Here's her number, and btw she needs a friend right now, even more than a booty call.

She sends me over her contact information, and I add it to my phone before putting it on the charger for the day.

I can't be that person. I need to just let it sit for at least tonight.

> ME: Thanks, Grace, and just so you know, I can't cross that line.

I tell her this, but honestly, I'm not sure if I'm trying to convince myself or her.

Lying in bed, I stare at the ceiling. It's like Mila's number is yelling, "Call me, text me, FaceTime me. You know you want to. Stop being scared and just do it."

The woman makes me weak, and I'm not sure if I'll be able to stay away if I talk to her outside of the treatment room. But dammit, I want to see what will happen.

Picking up my phone, I find her contact faster than I should have.

> ME: Hey, are you awake?

> Mila (Sexy Driver): Um, who is this?

Shit, I probably seem like some crazy stalker just asking a question like that when it's after midnight.

> ME: Shit. Sorry, it's Chase, I should have led with that. (Facepalm)

(Text bubbles)

I watch as the text bubbles come and go before she finally texts back.

> Mila (Sexy Driver): (laughing emoji) Yeah, you may have wanted to lead with that. I normally just block those texts pretty quick.

> ME: Then why did you text back?

> Mila (Sexy Driver): Honestly...

> ME: Yeah.

> Mila (Sexy Driver): I'm bored out of my skull and wanted to see who it was.

> ME: Then I'm glad I didn't get the block.

> Mila (Sexy Driver): So what can I do for you, Chase?

Groaning, I roll over and unplug the phone from the charger. What can she do for me? That's a question I've been rolling around in my head since I first saw her at the race shop. Lying back on my pillow, I think of what to say.

> Mila (Sexy Driver): Wow, I must have stunned you to not comment. That's amazing.

> ME: Actually, I was just trying to think of something that wouldn't make me sound like a perv, if you must know. You make a statement like that and my mind kind of went elsewhere.

> Mila (Sexy Driver): (blushing emoji)

> ME: Can't sleep?

> Mila (Sexy Driver): Not really. My mind wants to go all night, and when I do finally fall asleep, I have flashbacks of the wreck. Plus, this cast doesn't make for the best positions to sleep.

> ME: Have you tried anything to help you wind down before bed so your mind can shut off?

> Mila (Sexy Driver): Yeah, they gave me some meds, but I don't think they work for very long. Why, did you have something in mind that could help?

Shit, is she flirting with me? Was that a window for me to flirt back? This could go either way. Old Chase would have just been fine with leaving that text as is. But this new dominant Chase has other ideas.

> ME: Oh, I have a few different ways I could get your brain to stop working.

> Mila (Sexy Driver): Why, Chase Bryant! (Devil emoji)

> ME: You have no idea, driver.

Just as I send the text, my FaceTime alerts me I have an incoming call. And whose name do I see but the sexy driver?

I answer the call faster than I care to admit and wait for her gorgeous face to come on the video feed.

"Hey," she says.

Damn, the woman is beautiful. Her dark hair is in a high bun, and from what I can see, she's wearing a thin tank top. The room is dark, and the only light is coming from the phone.

Chapter 15
Mila

When Chase texted me just a few minutes ago, I had no interest in FaceTiming tonight. I had been playing this stupid game on my phone, just trying to get my brain to relax. But now, with only just a few words, the man has me turned on, and I hit the FaceTime button before I could even think about it.

The second his blond hair and glasses come into view, my brain misfires. He's lying in bed, one arm propped up behind his head and his gorgeous chest on full display. Damn you, blond Clark Kent. Of course, you look even better without your shirt. Why did I think differently?

Because you wanted to keep him in the DO NOT TOUCH box! That's why you work together. In not so many words, he put that boundary there.

Clearing my throat, I try to form words.

Laughing just a small amount as he removes his glasses, he says, "To what do I owe the pleasure of a FaceTime, Mila? Don't get me wrong, I'm loving the view." He moves to sit back against the headboard.

Ugh, the man is gorgeous. It's like Thor and Superman made one person, and bam, Chase Bryant came out.

I try to move to sit back against my headboard, but I take just a little longer since the fucking cast is making my life its bitch right now.

"Just wanted to take you up on that offer to help me get some sleep, is all."

"Oh really? You think I can help?" he says with a smirk.

"You said you had a few ways to get to sleep. Figure it couldn't hurt now, could it?"

I watch as his face goes from sweet to serious in a second.

"Mila, you do not know what you're asking. If, and I mean *if*, I help you, that means we are crossing a line. Are you willing to cross that? Even if it means that for now, it's behind doors?"

"Why, Chase Bryant, are you asking me to be your dirty secret?"

"Oh, baby, you do not know how dirty I can be."

I blush just a little with the way his voice says that. Damn, just hearing Chase say that turns me on. I've never experienced arousal from a voice alone, but my body lights up when he says it.

"Mila, you're blushing right now. Something you want to tell me?"

Smiling, I shake my head.

Letting out a laugh, he says, "Your head may be shaking no, but your nipples in that thin tank top say otherwise."

Looking down at my breast, I curse my body. Damn that voice.

"Now, I'm going to ask you again. Do you want to cross this line?"

Nodding my head, I open my eyes to watch his green ones go dark.

"I need your words, driver. If this is going to work, I need you to tell me."

"Yes, Chase, I want to cross the line." The instant the words are out of my mouth, I see his eyes trail over my tank.

"Take your tank top off, Mila. I want to see those gorgeous tits I've been thinking about."

I pull the tank over my head and lie back against the headboard so that he can see what he wants.

"Damn, those tits are perfect—small pink nipples that make me want to suck on them, making you come with just my mouth.

Touch yourself, Mila. I want to watch you get yourself off thinking of me."

I've never been self-conscious of my body. Hell, I get myself off more than I'm sure the average woman does, but when Chase talks to me, I want to come undone just from his words alone. I'm so on edge that it won't take much before I am doing just what he wants.

I pinch my nipples just how I like when I hear a groan come from Chase.

"Do you like what you see, Chase? Does me playing with myself, knowing you can't touch, turn you on?"

Finally, I'm feeling a little like my old self at this moment. I'm used to being the one in charge in the bedroom. I know just what I want and how to get it.

"Does my dirty secret like to use toys when she gets herself off?" he asks, making me smirk just a little at what he wants to see.

I turn to reach into my top drawer. Luckily, I had thought to bring this with me when I moved into Grace's guest room. A girl can only go so long before needing a brief release. And who the hell knows how long it's going to be before I'm able to ride again, if you know what I mean?

I slide back against the headboard, making a show of my toy to Chase. I like this side of him and knowing I can act like a brat. But this side of Chase I didn't expect at all, and I'm getting more turned on the longer this little game goes.

"Show me how you play with that toy, Mila. Make yourself come. I want you to do it hard and fast. Don't slow down until you are coming all over it, imagining that it's my dick inside you, making you moan in pleasure." He says it in that deep timbre that has me getting even wetter, so I don't even need to pull my lube out to cover the toy.

Pushing the toy inside, I let out a moan that I'm sure if Grace were awake, she would hear. Hell, I've heard her and Matt more than I care to admit.

"Show me, Mila." I hear Chase's voice come from the phone that I propped on the nightstand. Turning the phone so that he can see just what I'm doing has me picking up speed. I am so turned on, knowing that he's watching me. It's not long before I feel my orgasm coming.

"That's such a sexy sight. Come for me. I want to see just how much you want me."

I'm pumping so hard with the toy that when my orgasm takes over, I can't help but scream. It's one of the most intense orgasms I've ever given myself. Sitting there for a few seconds, I get my bearings back and suddenly realize that I'm alone. Listening to Chase dominate me in that sexy voice was almost like he was next to me, and I guess, in one sense, he was.

Lying down, I grab the phone from where I placed it and see Chase looking just as smug as he can.

"Good night, Mila. Hope you sleep some tonight," he says before clicking off the FaceTime.

What the hell just happened? Did I really just come in front of Chase? Hello, Mila, what is wrong with you? That cannot happen again, I think to myself, just as sleep takes over my body.

THE WEEKEND IS UNEVENTFUL, and my mood is completely shit. I'm not at the race for the second week in a row now, and I'm stuck watching it from the couch. Grace saw my progress in therapy this past week and thought I might like a weekend away since the race wasn't a terrible drive, but I just couldn't bring myself to go. I didn't want the media to have a field day with me at the track or have to answer a million questions about how physical therapy is going or when I'm expected to be back. So I told Grace she should support Matt and that I would be fine alone for two days.

So here I sit, watching the race from the couch, eating a tub of butter pecan ice cream. Yep, that's what my life is right now—eating ice cream right out of the container.

I haven't heard from Chase since a few nights ago when he made me come by his voice, and that may be a good thing. Yeah, I said I wanted to be his dirty secret, but did I truly mean it, or was I just so turned on I would have said yes to anything he offered?

Ugh, I have got to get out of this house. I've only gone two places since I got home from Daytona: the doctor's office and physical therapy. Maybe if I sit out on the back deck, my mood will change. Grace and Matt have the perfect view of the lake. Granted, mine is pretty great, too, but the time Grace has put into making her deck so relaxing makes it hard to turn down.

Mental note: have Grace revamp my deck when she gets back so that I can enjoy my view as much as hers.

I spend the rest of the day lounging on the outside couch. Matt placed a TV out here, so I'm able to watch the race while I continue to eat the ice cream that I just can't put down.

Matt and Ryan both have decent runs, but neither pull out the win, so I guess that's something they are gonna talk about all week. Yay, fun times.

> Grace: Hey, girlie, I'm headed back to Charlotte in about an hour. Matt's grumpy as hell, so brace yourself.

> ME: Yeah, I watched the race. I wondered what mood he had when he didn't win.

> Grace: Yeah, it's normally not too bad, but still grumpy. Don't worry, some lake time always makes him feel better. (Winking emoji)

> ME: (laughing emoji) Didn't really need to know that.

> Grace: Like I didn't need to hear you scream a certain physical therapist's name a few nights ago. (Smiling emoji)

> ME: (facepalm)

I honestly thought she was just going to bypass that, and I wouldn't have to face the embarrassment of my orgasm via Facetime with Chase.

> Grace: That's what I thought. See you soon, Mila.

> ME: Be safe coming home.

Sitting my ice cream down, I go to stand up, putting my ass back in my chair to head toward my room for the night.

Chapter 16
Chase

The weekend flies by, and all I can do is think about Mila. Watching her come on FaceTime was one of the best things I have ever seen. I've jacked off more than I care to admit to that image since then.

When Monday rolls around, I have a huge smile on my face. Should I have called or texted her the next day? Yeah, but I'm also trying to keep the boundaries so neither of us feels like we can't work together when she comes in for treatment today.

"Chase, your first patient is here. She's sitting in the waiting area," one of the nursing staff states.

As I move from my desk, my phone vibrates.

> Mila (Sexy Driver): Just because you saw me come the other night doesn't mean you can be late for my therapy. (Winking emoji)

Laughing at the text, I head toward my patient.

"Why, Miss Michelson, I believe you are early. I wasn't expecting you until nine this morning," I say, winking at her as I push her toward our treatment room.

"Well, Mr. Bryant, I thought being on time might be a good thing for once," she says as I help her onto the table.

"Besides, I think my leg is healing a little more, so I wanted to see if I might try standing today."

"Mila, I'm not sure that's an option right now. You only had surgery less than two weeks ago. We still have to let that bone set another week at minimum."

"Are you fucking kidding me!" she shouts. I refuse to be confined to that chair for another two weeks. I'm on the verge of pushing my wheelchair off the pier and into the lake because of how bored I am. "You have got to give me something to do besides these small exercises."

"Look, we can explore the possibility of increasing your exercises slightly, but until the four-week mark, our options are very limited. As soon as the orthopedic doctors give me the okay, I'll have you walking as much as you can take."

I watch the utter defeat come over her face as I know she wasn't expecting this to be this slow of a process. That's the thing with athletes that I understand. They want to speed things along. Hell, I once had a client who cut his own cast off because it was taking too long, and he wanted to get back to the football field. Fortunately, the cast was due to be removed in a week, and the bone had healed, but it was still foolish of him to handle it himself.

Walking close to Mila, I grab her face in my hands to get her to look at me.

I never want her to feel that she can't show me the real person she is. Just from the few times I've been able to be around her, she holds a lot in, wanting no one to think that she's weak. Being in the male-dominated sport, I guess, had made her feel like she couldn't be.

"Mila, baby, open your eyes and look at me," I say in a gentle voice.

Once those chocolate eyes open, I can see the pain in them.

"Chase, I can't do this. Waiting is the hardest thing. I'm a driver; that's all I've ever wanted," she says, and that breaks my heart just a little more seeing her be this vulnerable.

Before I know what I'm doing, my lips are on hers. My body

ignites with a thousand lightning strikes. Wrapping my hand around her hair, I position her mouth just where I want it and take everything she is giving me. She doesn't pull away—just grips my shirt and pulls me closer. Within a short time, she opens up to me, and our tongues become tangled in one another, intensifying the heat of the kiss.

Just as she moves her hands down my chest, my brain finally catches back up to what I'm doing, and I pull away.

"I'm sorry, Mila, I shouldn't have done that. You are my patient, and we shouldn't have crossed that line." I take a step back.

"Chase, it wasn't like I stopped you," she responds with a smile.

Stepping into her space, I pull her hair back and kiss her hard one last time before walking out the door of the treatment room.

What the hell am I doing? She's my patient.

She needs a friend right now, Chase. Grace's statement rings in my head.

Mila

What the hell was that? Chase kissed me, and oh my god, what a kiss it was. That's what I have been missing all these years. The spark.

After sitting in the treatment room for what feels like forever, Chase finally comes back. But this time, he's focused. He doesn't look at me unless he's giving me my next exercise to do or to make sure that I'm okay with the instructions.

It's like he flipped a switch and turned into this robot.

An hour later, I see Grace come over to check in on my

progress, and Chase gives her an update, then leaves without even so much as a goodbye.

You know what? That's fine if he wants to play that card and be a dick. Well, I can play the bitch card just as hard. Game on, Mr. Bryant.

"Hey, Mila, I just spoke with Chase, and he said your therapy is going really well. We should be able to get you in an air cast soon, and then you'll be able to walk with some assistance," Grace says, helping me into my chair before spinning me around and heading toward the door.

The ride back to the house is quiet. Right now, my emotions are just a little too volatile, and I really don't want Grace to endure what I should only direct at Chase.

"Hey, why so quiet? I expected you to be excited about the news today."

"Yeah, it's amazing," I say with as much sarcasm as I can.

Pulling into the driveway, Grace puts the car in park and then turns to face me.

"Mila, talk to me. You were so excited about the progress this morning and the help that Chase has done. Now you look like someone just kicked the hell out of you and walked away."

Yeah, that's one way to put it. Chase is giving me a bit of whiplash.

"It's nothing, Grace, really. I'm just tired from the session. I'll be fine tomorrow."

She looks at me for a few moments before blowing out a frustrated breath when I don't give her anything else and gets out of the car to help me in the house.

Chapter 17
Mila

The next two weeks fly by. Chase is as cold as a fucking deep freeze and only giving me instructions and checking my pain level. It's like I'm just a regular patient. There's no sweetness or caring in his voice anymore.

Later in the week, I'm able to finally get the cast off and go into a walking boot. Since my ankle is still a little unstable, they thought I needed to be in this for another few weeks, which is fine with me. I'm able to take it on and off and finally can take a bath instead of a shower. So I'll take a walking boot anytime.

Walking into physical therapy feels a little different now. Grace doesn't have to fuss over me, and I can come and go when I need to.

"Hey, Mila, I wasn't expecting you today," Jasper says, raising his eyebrows at me. Guess the look on my face isn't the nicest one because the former Navy man backs up pretty quickly when he sees what direction I'm headed.

I have officially had enough of Chase Bryant and the shit attitude he's had toward me over the last few weeks. You would think he was the one with the broken leg and career in the toilet at the moment the way he's been acting.

Not bothering to knock, I swing the door to his office open and walk in.

Chase is on the phone, and as soon as he gets a look at me, his eyes go wide, and his mouth opens and closes like a fish. If I wasn't so aggravated at him right now, I might find it a little funny.

"Hey, let me call you back," he says to whoever is on the other end of the phone.

Slamming the door behind me, I walk over to his desk.

"Mila, what the hell is wrong with you?"

"What's wrong with me? You have got to be fucking kidding me. Okay, let's see."

I take a deep breath and try to calm down so I don't seem like a crazy stalker, but I'm not sure I'm going to. I lean over the desk so I can look at him at eye level.

"I am over the cold shoulder you have been giving me. You make me come on FaceTime, then ignore me for days. Then you kiss me and act like a ghost. So the next time you even think about getting close to me, you better be able to make good on any actions you intend.

"I don't surrender to any man. And I damn sure will not play this stupid push-pull you think we're doing.

"So hear me when I say this. When I come into this building, you are to help me get back into that race car. You are not to sweet-talk me or make me think I might be something special or even get extra time in the treatment room. Are we crystal clear, Mr. Bryant?"

He just stares up at me, those gorgeous green eyes looking back at me. Damn him for making me weak.

I stand back up, pivot on my good foot, and walk toward the door.

Chase

As soon as she pivots on her heel, I am out of my chair and barreling toward the door before she can even open it.

"Is that how you wanna play this, driver?" My hand rests on the door just as she tries to open it.

Her brat attitude just awoke the dom in me, and I can't take it back now.

Looking over her shoulder at me, I see her eyes go wide as she turns around.

Caging her in, I step into her space.

"You honestly think that I'm doing this on purpose? That I would willingly let you just walk away from me.

"Mila, let me clue you in on something just so we are crystal clear, as you said.

"One, I can't date you. At least not right now. You're my client. So when I kissed you, I had to walk away because I wanted to fuck you so hard that everyone would know you belonged to me. That you were MINE!

"Two, when I push you in treatment, it's to make you heal quicker, not because I think it's fun. I could think of other punishments that are way more fun than what happens in that room.

"So the next time I kiss you, it will be when you are naked and under me while you scream my name. Is that clear enough for you?"

I step back from her and motion for her to open the door, but she just stares at me like I'm some puzzle she can't figure out. Well, get in line, sweetness, because you are making me crazy, and I'm not sure how much longer I can follow rule one.

Chapter 18
Mila

When I came to Chase's office today, I never thought I would get the reaction that I did. I just wanted to tell him how I felt, and that would be it. Now I'm standing in front of this gorgeous man, ready to get on my knees for him.

Dammit, I shake my head and finally walk out of his office like the good, albeit sassy, person I am.

Three more weeks. That's how long I have to be in therapy with Chase. I can hold out three more weeks. But then, after those three weeks, we are going to see what happens next. Getting into the car, I shake my thoughts clear from what Chase just threw down for me in his office.

Later that day, after my very interesting conversation with Chase, I'm sitting on the couch watching qualifying. Grace went to the race with Matt this weekend since I'm more than capable of taking care of myself now that I don't have the cast on. She needed a weekend away from being a nurse, plus I needed time to just be alone.

Seeing the guys clock laps at Martinsville, I feel my jealousy getting worse the more I sit watching the TV. Matt looks to have the car to beat, but if I have learned anything by being with Matt and Ryan, Ryan is the silent but deadly racer. You won't see him coming until he's already at your back bumper, and then he's going to strike.

Two hours later, qualifying is finally complete, with Matt

taking the top spot and Ryan coming in a solid eighth place for Sunday's race.

Grabbing my phone, I pull up my text thread with Grace.

> ME: Tell Matt a great job on taking the pole.

> Grace: Oh, I will. (Winking emoji)

> ME: Wasn't talking about that pole, perv.

> Grace: What, he's got a great pole, is all I'm saying.

> ME: You forget we share a wall. I hear you on that pole.

> Grace: Haha, what're your plans for today?

> ME: May just sit around and watch TV.

> Grace: You know you can go out, right? You are not in that cast anymore.

> ME: Yeah, I know, but I'm not sure I wanna deal with the press.

> Grace: Go to the bar down the road. They leave us alone when we are there. And who knows, you might find a pole of your own. (Laughing emoji)

> ME: Thanks, Grace. (Facepalm emoji)

> Grace: Just be safe.

> ME: I will IF I decide to go.

I sit staring at the TV and flip channels for another hour

before I'm so bored that I can't sit still. Maybe Grace is right. I need to get out of this house.

A little later, I've changed into a cute romper, and my hair is fixed. I want to have that drink. It's just a little walk from the house, and a girl's gotta eat.

Walking into the bar, Grace was right. Not a single person looks my way as I head toward the open seat at the corner of the bar.

"What can I get you?" the very cute bartender asks me once he notices I've sat down.

"Vodka tonic, please."

"Coming right up."

A few minutes later, he places my drink in front of me, along with a menu.

"Thought you might want something to eat," he says with a wink as he goes to help the couple at the end of the bar, who look like they can't function without one another's arms around each other. I can't help but laugh a little to myself at the sight of it. It seems as if they are joined at the hip.

"This seat taken?"

My body instantly goes on high alert. Of all the god-forsaken bars to be at.

Turning in my seat, I face the one man I do not want to be seeing right now.

"Actually, it is," I tell him as I take a sip of my drink and look over the menu.

"Doesn't look like it, sweetness," he says, coming close to my ear, making goosebumps break out on my skin with that deep timbre in his voice just as he sits down beside me.

"What do you want, Chase? Did you not take what I said to heart in the office?"

"Oh, I heard everything you said, and did you hear what I said?"

"I was just in the area, and Matt was talking about this place. It just happens that you're here as well."

Blowing out a frustrated breath, I try to decide what I want to eat. Since I'm here, I might as well grab something. Damn, I'm gonna need something stronger if Chase stays beside me. Wait, no, I better not drink. I'll do something stupid like ask him to make good on his promise earlier.

Looking at my menu, I hear him let out a little laugh. When I glare his way, I see him smiling at me.

"What, Chase? Am I amusing you now?"

He takes a pull of his beer, sets it down, and turns my barstool to face him.

"Is the menu that hard to read, or are you trying to just not look at me?"

Rolling my eyes, I turn my chair back and figure out what I want to eat.

Chapter 19
Chase

Never in a million years did I think I would run into Mila—tonight of all nights, especially after our little interaction earlier today.

Looking over my menu, I laugh at how hard Mila is trying to not look at me.

She had placed her order to go, and since then, I have watched her scroll through the same article three times now. I never thought I would make a woman nervous, but I guess things can change.

Reaching over to grab her phone, which evidently has an equation to solve global warming, I finally get her to look at me. She doesn't care about me turning her stool toward me, so I'm gonna have to try another way.

"Chase, give me my phone," she says, her teeth gritting together so hard I think she may chip one.

"Nope, you're going to sit here and talk to me."

"And why would I do that? You made it pretty clear the boundaries in your office, so don't come at me like you want anything other than nothing."

"Sweetness, I don't think you were paying attention then. I said I couldn't right now. Not that I didn't want to at all."

"It's easier to just see you in the office than outside, where I want to do things I can't, Chase. So please, just leave me alone, okay?"

I hand her phone back to her and just look at her for a moment. Pushing a stray hair behind her ear, I finally get those deep-chocolate eyes on me.

"Mila, I'm trying to be a good guy here. Can't you see that? I don't want people to think I fall for my patients. I need to be a professional. I worked too hard to get where I am, and in sports medicine, no less."

"Chase, I'm not asking you to break your rules, at least not right now. But I am asking you to think about it." She says this just as her food comes up in a to-go bag. She's leaving.

Giving the bartender her card, I know I only have a little longer with her before she's gone.

When she gets her card back, she places it in her pocket and goes to leave.

I stand up, throw a twenty on the bar, and reach for her arm.

"Let me walk you to your car."

Looking up, she smiles.

"I didn't drive; I just live around the corner. Well, actually, I'm staying at Grace's, but my house is just a few doors down from her."

"Then let me walk you home."

"Trying to be my knight in shining armor, Chase Bryant?"

"Something like that. Come on, Mila."

Grabbing her takeout bag, we head toward the door.

"Seriously, Chase, I can walk myself home."

"Mila, it's after ten at night. I'm not about to let you walk alone. You know as well as I do people disappear all the time and are never heard from again. I can't in good conscience let you walk alone."

"Fine, I live this way." She motions toward the lake drive just down from the bar.

When she finally gives in and starts walking, I breathe a sigh of relief. Damn, this woman is stubborn.

"So, Chase Bryant. Tell me a little about you," she says.

Ummm, okay. I look over at her as we continue down the path.

"Might as well get to know each other a little better, right? It's not like we really have time to talk during therapy. Plus, if we are going to do this friend thing, I need to know who Chase Bryant really is," she says, smiling up at me.

"Well, I grew up in North Carolina and went to school at Appalachian State. Then, PT school soon after. And I have been working at Jasper's clinic ever since I finished. He was the first place I interviewed when I got done with school, and we just clicked."

"Did you always want to help athletes?" she asks as we continue walking toward the townhomes on the lake.

"Yeah, I knew I wanted to do something in sports medicine. I played baseball in college. Nothing serious, just rec ball, but I've always been a part of the athletic world."

"Is that how you met Tinley?" That stops me in my tracks.

"She told me," she says, looking down at the gravel road as we get closer to the house.

Stopping her in the road, I turn her to face me because I need her to hear what I'm about to say.

"I know it's odd that Tinley and I have history, and I get it if that makes you uncomfortable. But we only went on one date, and I'm not even sure it was that, seeing as she kissed Ryan that same day as I was waiting for her in the stands. She's a brilliant woman, but I also watched the press have a field day with her over it. So if you're worried about what they might say about you and me, then don't. I have no interest in becoming a part of that world. I love being on the outside."

Her gorgeous brown eyes look at me as if I've just told her the sky was falling.

"Chase, it's not about Tinley. When I look at you, I see the possibility of what could be. And I think that scares me more than I want to admit. I see someone who, if I let him in, has the power to hurt me. Chase, I'm already so broken from the wreck

I'm not even sure my mind will let me get into a race car without having a panic attack. So when I say I'm not looking to get involved, I really, truly am serious."

She continues. "So yeah, we can't date, and honestly, that may be a blessing. You don't want someone who's trying to figure out if she still fits into the world she loves. Do I want to kiss you and talk to you and even have sex with you? Yeah, I do, but I'm not sure I can give you all the things a girlfriend could."

Dropping her arm, I can't help but deflate just a little. I thought with the walk home and talking that we were making progress. She was opening up a little. But I guess that's what I get for thinking there might be something more here.

If she needs a friend, I'll be that. If she wants just a physical therapist, then I'll be that… even if it kills me.

"I get it, Mila." I hand her takeout bag to her and stop one last time to look at the beautiful woman. "I'll see you for therapy in a few days." Then I head back toward the bar.

She put me in the friend zone before I even had a chance with her. But little does she know, I'm not giving up without a fight. She needs to heal from the crash, and then I'm going to be there every step of the way… inside and outside of the therapy office.

Chapter 20
Chase

Mila saying she wasn't ready to see what we could be had me thinking. Maybe if I can help her heal from the crash, she might just see I'm worth the effort. So I have come up with a treatment plan that I think she might like just as much as being in the actual car.

"Grace, why are we here? I have to be at the therapy session in ten minutes, and it's all the way across town." I hear Mila talking to Grace coming down the hall.

"Mila, will you just trust me? This is where you are supposed to be today for therapy," Grace says as they come into the simulation room.

I'm standing by the driver's seat when Mila's beautiful form comes into view. Damn this woman.

"Chase, why are we here?" she asks with surprise.

"Thought we might have a change of pace today. See how that leg and ankle feel on the pedals?"

She looks at me like I've just given her the keys to winning every race in the cup series. She comes hobbling over to me, and, to my surprise, she jumps into my arms, wrapping her arms around my neck.

"Chase, you do not know how much I needed this today," she says, giving me a small kiss on the cheek before letting go of my neck and heading to the seat.

Mila works on adjusting the seat so that she can get in with her boot on. Then she types in her information to get the machine running with the next racetrack they will head to.

"Now, Mila, what I need you to do is drive like you don't have the boot on. I need to know how the ankle and leg are feeling, especially when you are switching gears. That's going to be very important in what adjustments we make in the coming weeks. Because we want to get you back to practicing in an actual stock car in two weeks, so the boot will come off next week."

"Okay, so just drive like I don't have an extra five pounds on my leg. It sounds so easy." She says this with the sass I am starting to really enjoy.

I watch as she changes gears in the simulator. Her face is so serious that if I wasn't looking for any signs of pain, I might have missed them. The subtle changes when she goes to change gears. She has more issues with starting in the gear change than when she has been racing a little bit. But what I didn't expect happens midway through the session.

It's like I'm watching something happen in slow motion. One second, Mila is going through the motions; the next, she's spinning out in the simulator car and having a panic attack.

I'm on my feet faster than I can even think and jerking her out of the car.

"Mila, Mila, look at me. It's fine. It's just a simulator. You're not in the car. I'm here. Take a deep breath for me," I say, trying to get her to focus on me.

Watching Mila have a panic attack was not the reaction I thought I was going to get out of today.

She may like others to think she's okay—hell, until this point, I was thinking the same thing—but this reaction to the race just makes me worry even more about her getting back into that stock car.

Chapter 21
Mila

My vision is blurry, and the ringing in my ears is still so loud. What the hell just happened to me? One moment, I'm practicing in the simulator, and the next, I'm in Chase's arms, with him trying to get me to breathe.

"Baby, breathe for me. You need to calm down, okay?" I hear him say.

As I try to take another breath, the ringing stops, and I can slowly make out Chase's face.

"That's it. Take another one for me," I hear him say again, so I do as he instructs.

"Mila, Mila, are you okay?" I hear Grace say. Her voice is softer than it normally is.

"What happened?" I finally find my voice as I look up to Chase.

"You had a panic attack, Mila. I'm so sorry. I didn't think that would cause a reaction like this with you being in the simulator."

Reaching up to cup his face, I can see how concerned he is. This beautiful man was worried about me.

"Guess I'm not ready for the track just yet, huh, Mr. Bryant?" I say with a smirk, and that finally gets a smile from him.

"Miss Michelson, I think we still have some work to do before I will let you get in an actual car, that's for sure."

Chase helps me stand up as Grace brings a bottle of water over so that I can try to get my head around what just happened.

I have never had a panic attack before, let alone when I have been in a car. This is just one other obstacle I am going to have to get over, and dammit if I don't want to conquer it today!

"Set the sim back up, Chase. I wanna go again."

"Mila, I'm not so sure we should. That was a scary-as-hell panic attack."

"Set it up again." I say it a little more aggressively so he knows it's not up for discussion.

"I am not backing down to a panic attack, Chase. I may not drive my actual car right now, but I'll be damned if this is going to happen when I get my car back. So, like I said, set the machine up again."

It takes three more tries and two mini panic attacks before I'm able to push past the barrier that my brain had decided it wanted to live in, but I was able to finish an entire session in the machine.

My ankle hurts like a bitch, but I did it. I showed I was stronger than most and that I want my car back sooner rather than later.

"Alright, Mila, that's plenty for today. Make sure you ice that ankle because it's going to be swollen from the amount you used it today, and I'll see you at the clinic in a few days."

Limping over to Chase, I look at him in a different light now. The man saw I was struggling but never once told me I couldn't do it. Hell, he took care of me in a full-blown panic attack. Maybe he is worth taking a chance on. Just maybe.

Reaching up, I kiss Chase and walk away.

A FEW HOURS LATER, I'm lying on the couch with Matt and Grace, watching a movie, when my phone pings.

> Chase: Want to clue me in on that kiss earlier today? Thought you wanted to be just friends.

> ME: Well, I do, but maybe when you take care of a person when they are struggling, that deserves something extra.

> Chase: Baby, I can take care of you extra. All you have to do is say the word.

A smile crosses my face, which seems to get Grace's attention.

"And just what made you smile like that? Just who are you texting, Mila?" She wiggles her eyebrows at me.

"No one. It's nothing." I put my phone down and turn my attention back to the movie Matt chose.

"Yeah, I know that look. It wouldn't be the blond Clark Kent, would it?" she asks, looking at me like she can read my mind.

"I don't know who you're talking about," I say, laughing just a little at the face Matt gives her.

"Blond Clark Kent—who the hell is that, Red?" Matt asks, looking at her before moving back to the TV.

"Wanna tell him, Mila, or should I? Because I knew after seeing you both today, you're trying to play it off as nothing, but it really is something."

Blowing out a long breath, I sit up a little more on the couch.

"Fine, it's Chase. Okay, happy, Mom?"

Laughing, she smacks Matt. "See, I told you I would get it out of her."

"Are you kidding me right now, Grace? Leave the woman alone." Matt says, still watching the movie like we are bothering him from watching something he has seen a million times.

"Give me all the details, Mila. I need to know."

Ugh. I throw my body back onto the pillow again. "Can we just not right now, Grace? Honestly, I'm not even sure what the hell is going on. When we are together, it is so hot and cold."

"Well, seeing y'all together in the sim lab today was pretty much in the tropical zone. He even took care of you when you had a panic attack."

"Wait, you had a panic attack in the lab today, Mila?" Matt is now fully paying attention to our conversation.

"Yes, I did, and Chase helped me through it. I tried the sim a few more times, and by the end of the day, I had them under control."

"That's still pretty serious, Mila. What if it happens when you get in a real stock car?"

"Matt, I said I've got it under control, okay? I think when the time comes, I'll be fine with the real thing."

"Okay, just if you freak out, don't get out on that asphalt. That's all I'm saying." And he goes back to watching his movie.

"So, are you going to see him outside of the clinic?"

"Ugh, you're like a dog with a bone, aren't you, Grace?"

"Give me some details, and I'll leave you to text your superhero."

"Yes, I like Chase! Are you happy?" I say, throwing the pillow over my face and wanting to fall into a dark hole.

Chapter 22
Chase

Mila kissed me. She kissed me and actually smiled as she walked away. Granted, it could have been because I helped with the panic attack, or it could have been that she finally saw me as more than a friend. Guess that's why I'm sitting here wondering what, if anything, she will text back after I replied to her a few minutes ago.

I was out on a walk with Miller when my thoughts kept going back to that moment in the sim room. Could she actually want to move from the friend zone she put me in just a few nights ago?

Just as I get Miller's food set down, my phone lights up.

> Mila (Sexy Driver): I'm sure you can deliver on any ideas.

I'm getting ready to text her back when my statement comes rushing at me.

Client, she's a client. Tread carefully.

> Mila (Sexy Driver): Wanna meet for drinks in a little?

> ME: That sounds friendly enough.

> Mila (Sexy Driver): See you at the bar shortly, you know the one.

I look at the text and can't believe what is happening. Mila just asked to meet for drinks. Well, damn, I better get a shower.

An hour later, I'm pulling into the bar just down from Mila's house. As I'm getting out of the car, I hear a certain voice that I am loving more and more come from behind me.

"Bryant, took you a long enough." The woman is drop-dead gorgeous in just a simple pair of cutoff jean shorts and a dark-green tank.

Walking up to me as I lock my door, she wraps her arms around my neck.

"Well, Miss Michelson, I had a little farther to come," I say, placing my arms around her waist and bringing her closer to me.

"Wanna tell me why I'm here?" I ask, coming close to her ear, making her break out in goosebumps.

She removes her arms from around me and takes a step back, motioning me to follow her.

"Actually, I wanted to talk to you, and doing it over the phone just doesn't work for me, if you must know," she says, walking toward the bar.

Once we sit at a table toward the back of the bar and get our drinks, I'm more on edge than I should be.

Damn, it's been a long time since I've been on a date. Shit, is that what this is? Or is it just friends getting drinks and talking about their day? I'm gonna need this woman to talk, and fast, before I open my mouth.

Blowing out a breath, she takes another drink of her vodka tonic and finally looks at me.

"Okay, what I'm about to say I don't say because of what happened today. We may have something here, and as much as I want to leave you in a box and walk away, my heart says that I should see what it is. But that is also the reason I don't want to. You make me nervous, Chase. You make me want things I don't need. The distraction that could make me less of who I am. It's dangerous to be with me, to fall in love with me, Chase. I may hurt you because my career comes first. I can't promise I'll be around like you might need. But the pull to you is more than I can stand anymore, even with the push-pull that we do. I know I said we needed to be friends, and that was less than a week ago. But after what you did for me today, I can't put you in that box anymore.

"Every time we are together, I know you feel the electric current just as much as me.

"The day you kissed me in the treatment room and then rushed out, I know you felt it. I've fought it as much as I could. So, with that long rant, Chase Bryant, would you like to date me?"

I sit in the booth looking at this strong woman, the woman who has laid out just how she's feeling and making sure I'm aware of the life she leads, and I am in awe.

She makes liking her easy once she lets you into her circle, and I'm sure if she lets me, she will be even easier to love one day.

Laughing just a little at the information that Mila gave me, I can't help but look at her for a beat.

"Mila, you make it easy to say yes when you lay it out just like that. Honestly, I would have waited a lot longer if I had to. If I had known that taking you to that simulation room would cause a panic attack, I would have done it sooner to make you see me as more than just a friend or even the person who is helping you rehab," I say, reaching out to grab her hand.

"Baby, you had me before you even knew you did."

With that statement, she jumps out of her seat and launches herself into my arms.

She fits perfectly with me, and I am never letting her go.

"Kiss me, Chase Bryant."

"Baby, you sure you want me to make this so public?"

"Yes, I want everyone to know that I'm taken. I know you hate being in the spotlight, but we may have to fix that. And hate to break it to you, but you're coming to the races with me once I'm back in that car, and the world is going to know that I have the sexy blond Clark Kent on my arm."

She wiggles a little in my arms. "And in my bed," she adds in such a sexy voice I lose all control and crash my mouth onto hers.

Chapter 23
Mila

The second Chase's mouth connects with mine, I'm a goner. The man is so sweet and respectful until he's not. And let me tell you, right now, I am here for it.

Pulling away from his kiss, I just stare at his perfect face. The dark-green eyes, the light dusting of freckles across his button nose, and the slight scruff he has from not shaving this morning before work. I just take it all in—putting them all away in my memories that are only Chase.

"Wanna get out of here, Chase?" I ask before my brain thinks otherwise.

The man has played in a million and one of my fantasies over the last few weeks, and dammit, I'm tired of waiting. If he wants to do this, then I'm jumping in with both feet.

Putting me back down on the ground, he stands and places some cash on the table before turning to walk toward the door.

We only got to have one drink and no dinner, which was the plan when I asked him to meet me here. But my mouth got away from me, and now my lady parts are taking over, and I can't sit here any longer with this sexy man in front of me.

Grabbing my hand, he walks us toward his car.

"Your place or mine, driver?" he asks in that deep voice that makes my brain shut off.

"Mila, I need your words, sweetheart. If we are going to do this, I need you to talk to me and tell me what you want."

I clear my throat and get my head on straight for a moment, then reach over to have him look at me. "Mine."

With a smirk, he puts the car in drive and, like he's been to my house a million times, he parks in front of the door, puts the car in park, and gets out. Making his way around the front of the car, he comes to help me out of the passenger side.

He closes the door behind me as I get out and backs me up against the door, caging me in. Then he runs his hand up my leg and under my shirt before coming to rest on my lower back.

It may be one of the hottest moves I've ever had from a man before, and if I were wearing underwear right now, they would be soaking wet.

"You're turned on right now, aren't you, Mila? I can smell you from here, and it's making me hard just touching you." His lips come to graze my ear before sucking on that magical spot just below my neck.

Arching into his touch, I can't help the small moan that comes from my lips.

His kiss this time is gentle, like he's teasing me.

"Show me where your bedroom is, baby," he says, stepping back from me.

Grabbing my keys from my pocketbook, I walk up the steps and put an extra little sway in my walk as I go.

It's hard to think that it's been over four weeks since I was home. Grace and Matt have turned into my family. I knew that the time was coming to move back here, and I guess having Chase here is just what I need to feel at home again.

I hear the door close behind me and the lock click.

Setting my things down on the bar, I feel Chase come up behind me, wrapping his arms around me and kissing my neck. The move is so intimate it makes my heart swell just a little more for the man who is coming to mean a lot to me.

"I think I said show me to your room, driver. This is the living room."

Spinning around, I look up to see Chase with that smirk on his face that I've noticed he gives when he's trying to get what he wants.

Okay, two can play this game.

"Well, Mr. Bryant, the bedroom is just down the hall," I say as I remove my tank and throw my shirt at him and head down the hall.

I hear what I think is a growl from him, followed by heavy footsteps just before I am launched into the air and thrown over Chase's shoulder.

"You're a brat, you know that?" he says right before smacking my ass so hard I let out a yelp.

"Tell me one thing, Mila. Do you always act like that, or is that just for me?"

Giggling just a little, I can't help but think about what he really wants to hear.

"Oh, I'm a brat when I want to be. You just seem to bring it out a little more, Mr. Bryant."

I hear him growl again as I'm thrown onto the bed. With my ankle in the boot, I'm able to move a little easier than I would have been able to in a cast, which, at this moment, I am so thankful for.

"I can't promise I'll be gentle, Mila. Honestly, with sex, I have a certain taste, shall I say." He says this with his eyes daring me to question him as he comes to loom over me.

"The quiet ones are always the ones who come with rules, Mr. Bryant. So tell me what your tastes are, and maybe I can give you what you want," I sass.

He moves his hands down my stomach and toward my jean shorts, then looks back up to me.

"Maybe another night. Tonight, I just want to fuck you and have you screaming my name, just like I promised you would do the other day."

Slowly unbuttoning the first button, he pushes them down my legs.

"Is this what you had in mind when you asked me to meet you tonight, driver? Is that why you're not wearing panties for me, Mila? Did it turn you on having your shorts rub your clit while you walked to me at the bar tonight?" he asks just as he blows on my swollen clit.

"Oh god, Chase, yes, do that again."

"Baby, I'm just getting started."

Unhooking my bra as he teases me, I wrap my hand around his hair just as he licks my pussy.

When I buck up on the bed, he grabs one of my breasts.

"I've been thinking about these tits since the night you showed me how you get off on the phone." He squeezes just a little before playing with my already hard nipple.

"Yes, Chase, please don't stop." I moan as he plays with my other breast.

The man knows just what he's doing, and the more he licks and sucks my clit into his mouth, the closer I am getting to coming. It feels unreal.

I reach again to put him just where I need him, only to have a growl come from his chest.

"Mila, I'm getting ready to tie you to that bed if you don't let me eat you as long as I want. I don't care how many times you come. Your pussy is perfect, and I intend to enjoy it."

A gasp comes from my lips as he bites down on my clit, making my hand move from his hair.

"Yes, sir," I say.

That statement seems to get his attention, and he looks up at me.

He climbs up my body and kisses me. It's hot and needy, and I can taste my arousal on him. I grind against him with such need that I am going to make myself come if he doesn't stop me.

"Mila, stop moving," Chase says in a very dominant voice. I instantly react to his command.

Moving back from me, I watch as he pulls a condom from his wallet taking his pants and underwear in one swoop then puts the condom on his perfect dick.

Damn this man. Smart, sexy, and the perfect dick. How the hell is he still single?

"On your knees, Mila. You think you can do that?"

"Yes, sir," I say again. Where the hell is this "yes, sir" coming from? It's like I have no other words but those for him.

I roll onto my knees, just as he asked, my ankle hanging over the edge of the bed so that I'm not putting pressure on it. As soon as I'm comfortable, Chase comes to stand behind me.

Wrapping his arms around my waist, he plays with my breast before moving his hand down to my clit. I am so turned on by this man that I can't even make words out when he slams into me.

"Damn, Mila," I hear him say when he fucks me.

"So fucking perfect, just like I thought you would be."

"Chase, yes, Chase."

"You like that, Mila? You like it rough like that?"

"Yes, Chase. Fuck me harder. I can take it. I won't break."

And he fucks me harder. The second his finger slides across my clit, I come hard. So hard I think my legs may give out.

Just as I'm coming down from my orgasm, I feel Chase slam into me one more time before finding his release.

We stay in this position for a few minutes, both trying to catch our breaths. Then Chase finally pulls out and goes toward the bathroom to dispose of the condom.

I'm lying on the bed trying to get my bearings when he comes back with a glass of water and a warm washcloth to make sure that I'm clean.

"You need to drink this water, Mila."

"Yes, sir."

Dammit, brain. You know over two words. Why aren't you working?

Laughing at my response, he comes to sit beside me. He makes sure I drink the glass of water he brought for me, and then he sighs.

"Mila, I need to tell you something."

"Chase, we really don't need to right now. Let's just live in our post-orgasm bubble for a little."

"It's something that you need to be aware of before we go any further, okay? And you can walk away before we get too deep in this."

"Chase, gotta say you're freaking me out just a little."

He takes a deep breath and then talks.

"Mila, I like to dominate my partner sometimes and not always in the bedroom."

I'm sure my face shows complete shock right now.

"Chase, you're gonna have to repeat that for me because I think I just heard you say you like to be a bit of a dom, like *Fifty Shades of Gray* dom," I say with a small giggle.

"Well, I am, and when you say, 'Yes, sir,' it brings out that side in me. I just want you to know that in bed, I don't always like simple sex. I want the extras that come with being in that lifestyle again—not all the time, but sometimes I might want to try things. If you're up for it," he says, reaching for my hand.

"Do you have this need all the time? Like if I were to go into your bedroom, would I find toys in some secret room?"

"Yes, I have some toys; I don't like to punish my partners. I'm more into the pleasure side of it. I just want you to have all the information in case I ask you to try it one night. I didn't want you to be surprised. It's not something I expect, but I do enjoy it."

"Thank you for being so honest with me, Chase. And I am a little intrigued by the idea of having fun in the bedroom. I've always been the one in charge, so it will be a pleasant change."

"Well, the brattiness you have sometimes doesn't surprise me at all." He smirks, bringing me close to wrap me in his arms.

And I fall asleep in his arms.

Chapter 24
Chase

Waking up the next morning, I can't help the smile that comes on my face. After Mila fell asleep in my arms, I drifted off soon after, sleeping better than I have in a long time.

Kissing the top of her head and trying to be as quiet as I can, I get up, trying to find my clothes as I go.

After a quick trip to the bathroom and looking back over at Mila to make sure she's still sleeping, I slip out of the bedroom in search of the coffee maker. The sun is just coming up over the lake, and I take in the beautiful view that she has from her kitchen.

I'm standing in the kitchen when I hear her soft footsteps come to stand in front of me.

"You left me all alone in that enormous bed. What are you doing up so early?" she asks, her voice a little raspy. She's wrapped up in a blanket, and her raven hair is pulled up in one of those knots on her head.

Kissing the top of her head, I just look at her for a moment. The woman is just gorgeous. How the hell did I get so lucky to have her?

"What are you thinking, Chase?"

I smile down at her, give her a small peck, and then move to the coffeepot to grab two coffee cups.

"You make it easy to fall for you, Mila."

"Haha, I think if I would have asked you that a few weeks ago, you may have given me a completely different answer."

"Nope, it would have been the same. I was just waiting for you to take me out of the friend zone."

"I'd say you're way out of that zone now."

I hand her a cup of coffee and motion for her to follow me.

"I ordered some food for us since it looks like you have nothing in this house to eat."

"Yeah, since the accident, I've been staying with Grace and Matt. This is the first time I have been back at my house since I left for Daytona, actually. Guess I need to go shopping soon, huh?" she says with a small laugh, following me to sit out on her deck.

"Don't worry, baby, we can go to the store later."

"Really trying to woo me with the simple things, aren't you, Mr. Bryant?"

"Sometimes, it's not about the big gestures; it's about the simple things that people take for granted. Going to the grocery store is just one of them."

We sit out on the deck for a little longer before the doorbell rings, and I jump up to go grab our food.

Not really knowing what Mila likes for breakfast, I just ordered a few things that anyone would love. Pancakes, yogurt, bacon, toast, and, of course, you can't go wrong with more coffee.

Just as I'm getting things set up, I see Mila get up from her seat outside to come and join me for breakfast.

This is the life that I want. Maybe, just maybe, if I'm lucky, she'll want it too.

An hour later, we are both stuffed from the amount of food we consumed. I was starving this morning since we both forgot about supper when we got back to the house last night.

When I stand up to clear the plates, Mila stops my movement.

"Thank you for this, Chase. Last night and this morning have been more than I could have ever asked for. You have been so patient with me the last few weeks, and I know I still have a little therapy left, but you have made me see what the other side of this looks like, and I'm ready for it."

Leaning down, I tip her chin up to look at me.

"Mila, I would have tried everything to get you back in that car faster if I could. But I also wanted to take my time because that meant I got to spend more time with you." I pick her up into my arms and lay her back onto the table.

I could kiss this woman every second of every day. My body seems to heat with electricity every time we are around one another.

I'm so focused on Mila and what I have in mind for her that neither of us hears the front door open.

"Whoa," and "Dammit, Grace, I told you we should have just called her." I hear Matt's voice break through my Mila-induced haze.

Breaking our kiss, I look up just as Grace crashes into the back of Matt.

"Ouch. What the hell, Cowboy? Don't stop in the doorway. I need to make sure that Mila is okay."

"Yeah, Red, I think she's just fine," Matt says, motioning for her to walk around him.

Grace stops dead in her tracks when she sees Mila on the kitchen table.

I can't help but laugh at the sight she must see. Plates are scattered on the table, and Mila is laughing while pressing her face into my chest as I stand in front of her.

"Yes, Grace, I am one hundred percent good. Sorry I didn't call last night. I, umm, was a little busy." Mila's cheeks turn a shade of red that I hope to get to see more of.

"Oh, I see that now." Turning on her heels, she grabs Matt's arm and walks back out the door they just came from.

"You better call or come over later, heifer. We have a lot to talk about," Grace says as the front door closes behind them.

Mila breaks into a fit of laughter as I go to stand up, pulling her with me and placing her feet on the ground.

"Let's get this cleaned up." I kiss her one more time before I grab the plates and takeout containers.

Chapter 25
Mila

After we got the kitchen cleaned up, Chase gave me one last kiss before heading home. When he said he needed to check on his dog, Miller, I couldn't help but swoon a little. I have always loved dogs but never had time for one with my schedule, so knowing that he has one makes my heart happy.

A few hours later, I'm getting changed, putting my boot on, and heading out the back door toward Grace's house. I knew she would only give me so long before she came knocking. But damn, the girl had some timing, that's for sure.

Just as I get to the back deck of Grace and Matt's house, I smell steak on the grill. I gotta hand it to Matt—the man can cook. And that's a good thing for Grace because, unfortunately, I have been on the receiving end of her attempts to cook while Matt was gone one weekend, and let me tell you, it was rough.

"Nice of you to put some more clothes on, Mila," Matt says with a smirk.

"Ugh, can we just not, Cowboy? It's bad enough y'all let yourself into my house. Luckily, I was still wearing all my clothes."

I laugh a little as I walk past him and head toward Grace.

"If it isn't the one and only Mila," Grace says as I come into the living room where she's sitting with Tinley.

"Hey, let me see your phone really quickly." She reaches her hand out.

"Why the hell do you need my phone?"

"Just hand it over," she says with an unreadable mask on.

Handing it over, she looks at it. Then, being the smart-ass she is, she pulls her phone out and presses the call button.

I stand there for a second, then sit down in the oversized chair across from her and watch her be very dramatic, having a conversation with herself.

"Hello, Mila. Oh, hey, Grace."

"Yeah, I'm good. I'm at home with Chase."

"Well, that's great. Thanks for letting me know you're not staying with me tonight."

"No problem."

"See you tomorrow. Yep, I'll see you later."

Rolling my eyes, I look over at Tinley, who is about to pee her pants. She's laughing so hard at the show Grace has just put on.

"Tinley, you are not helping my cause right now."

"I'm sorry. It's just so funny to see her do the impression of you because it's pretty spot on," she says, still laughing.

Grace tosses my phone back to me and breaks out into a fit of laughter.

"I'm just picking on you, Mila. You're a grown-ass woman, and you can do as you please, just as long as I don't have to do damage control."

I stand up from the chair and walk toward the kitchen to grab a glass of wine, turning around to look at Grace.

"I can promise I'll keep my private life private. I have no interest in putting Chase on show, that's for sure."

"That's good because just from knowing Chase from back in college, he wants nothing to do with the media, especially after the Tinley and Ryan triangle that he almost became."

"Don't listen to her, Mila. Chase was never a part of any triangles," Tinley says, reassuring me.

A FEW HOURS LATER, I'm walking back to my house and wondering what Chase did today.

Did he have a good afternoon?

Has he thought of me?

Am I going to see him again outside of the treatment area?

When I walk back into the house, I'm greeted by a smell that most girls could only dream of.

Looking around my living room, I see flowers. And not just a dozen or two, but twelve or fifteen dozen. My living room looks like a million flowers have taken up roots and made it their home.

As I'm walking around the gorgeous arrangements, I finally get to the card that is sitting in the middle of the circle of flowers.

Mila,

Flowers may say a million different things, but I wanted them to say just how amazing you are, and taking the leap may just be the change you needed to take but didn't want to because of fear.

I'm glad you took it.

xoxo

Chase

(PS. Thank Matt for letting me in the house to arrange all these flowers)

I have never been a very romantic girl. Hell, I drive a car at two hundred mph every weekend. But I gotta say, a girl could get used to being treated like a princess.

Pulling up my text message chain with Chase, I send him a quick picture text and then head to bed.

The man just earned some bonus points, that's for sure.

Two weeks later, I'm finally able to get the boot off, and I couldn't be happier about it.

Chase has been the most amazing boyfriend, except for when we are at the clinic—then he is the definition of composed. I wish I could say the same. If I had it my way, he would have me in every unique position in this treatment room.

If you had told me two weeks ago that we would develop a relationship in private, but in public, people would never know, I would have told you that's absurd. You can't hide something like that. It's like the press knew the moment I was happy. Some beacon in the night calling out to them.

"Okay, Mila, we are going to do a few more exercises to make sure that your ankle and leg are ready for you to get in the car tomorrow. I'm going to have you use the rowing machine to test your strength, and you need to tell me if anything feels off," Chase says as we head toward the machine.

Sitting down on the seat, I get in position to make the rowing motion. And the instant I start the movement, I can tell my ankle is still a little tender but not unbearable. It may be because my ankle is stiff, so I do a few more reps like Chase instructs me. By the fifth turn, I am getting into the groove and can feel my ankle loosening up.

"Okay, Mila, you can stop. I've seen enough." He grabs his tablet to type something out.

Just as he hits send on the email for my crew chief, he turns toward me and smiles that beautiful smile. He has news for me that I'm either going to love or I'm going to absolutely hate in about two seconds.

"Spit it out, Bryant. The entire class wants to know why you are smiling like that," Grace says, becoming impatient with the dramatic wait.

"Believe me, it's one of two things," I say to Grace, who's standing with me, waiting for the news that I can train some on the track tomorrow.

"Well, with the exercise that you just did and watching your face while you did the motion, I could tell that the start was rough, but the longer you went, the more your face eased up. So I think you are ready to get back in the car."

Jumping to my feet, I rush over to Chase and crush my mouth to his. At this moment, I don't care who's around. Chase just gave me back my dream, and I can't wait to show him my world.

"Glad I could help, babe," Chase says, laughing as he sits me back down. He gives me one more quick kiss before telling us he has to get to his other patients.

I'm on cloud nine as we drive back toward the race shop. It feels like it's been an eternity since I could get in my car. Six weeks seems like a year ago. I have never taken a break from it since I started racing at a young age.

Pulling into Mac Motorsports a short while later, my whole body is humming with excitement.

As Grace and I walk into my crew chief's office, I find him looking more tense than normal. He's usually a happy-go-lucky guy, even when things aren't going as he might like.

"Hey, ladies, have a seat," he says as we go to sit in front of his desk. I see Grace grab her tablet out of her bag as I put my phone on silent.

"Alright, boss-man, tell me what we need to do to get my car ready for racing next week."

"Well, I got the email from Chase just a little while ago clearing you for racing, and our first stop will be to go out to Charlotte and race the track for a little. See how you're feeling. I know you haven't been able to really train and condition as much as normal since your leg has been out of commission, so that's the first thing. The second is we need to get the PR up and running again. I know Grace has kind of kept it going with updates here and there on the progress, which has been good, and also, the sponsors staying on helps."

"When we are out at the track tomorrow, Mila, we will get some promo stuff so that we can post on your Instagram and TikTok. Let them know you're back and ready to run," Grace says, typing away on her tablet, not even bothering to look up at me as she does it.

"Okay, sounds like a plan. I'm ready."

"Plan on being at the track at eleven in the morning. We have closed the track off so no one will be there but our team. Ryan and Matt will be there also, so they can give you a feel for other cars around you when running."

Getting up to stand, I can't help but be so excited. It's like Christmas morning, and I can't wait.

"Looks like we have a busy day ahead of us tomorrow, Mila. Time to get to work. I need you to be on the track before eleven. We will get some promo stuff done before racing," Grace says as we exit the office and head to where the cars are being set up for the next race.

As I walk into the garage, something settles inside me. I didn't even realize that I needed it. The past six weeks had me feeling every emotion in the book, and just smelling the fuel and oil helped click my mind back into place.

The next morning, I wake up extra early. After meeting with everyone at the shop yesterday, all the things that had been thrown at me completely wore me out, both mentally and physically.

I put on my leggings and tank top and head to the coffeemaker, knowing I'm gonna need the extra kick of caffeine. Today is going to be just as long.

Pulling the eggs and bacon out of the fridge, I make an omelet; making sure I have some food in my system is priority number one right now. I can't afford to appear weak at all. I need to show everyone I'm ready to run next week and that I'm back.

After finishing breakfast, I check all my socials as Grace instructed me to do. Then I grab a bottle of water and head toward the track.

Half an hour later, I'm pulling into Charlotte Motor Speedway.

Once I park and head toward my trailer, I see my baby. I could cry happy tears right now—not only for coming back from a wreck like I have but also because this team has been by my side the entire way.

"Ready to do this lady?" Grace asks as I get closer to where she is standing.

"You do not know how ready," I say, walking around my car, looking it over as I smile up at her.

"Well, go get changed, and let's get going before the guys get here and I lose you to racing."

Laughing just a little, I head toward the hauler to get my suit on.

Once I have my driving shoes laced up and my firesuit on, I head toward Grace. Being in this suit, I feel even more like myself. Don't get me wrong, I love dressing up, but this is the one place I feel like myself.

During the next two hours, I think Grace has made me walk the entire length of this damn track. From walking on the pit road looking like I'm ready to take on the world to putting my helmet on and getting in the car to just leaning against it.

So when she says we are finally done, I'm actually ready to jump in my car and drive as far from her as I can.

"Mila, nice of you to finally decide to come back to the track." I hear Matt laugh as he and Ryan walk toward my car.

"Just giving you boys something to do today. You know, since you need practice."

Ryan throws his head back, laughing. Matt and I have come to have a brother-sister relationship since living with him and Grace for those few weeks, and Ryan thinks it's the best thing.

"Nice to have you back, Mila. Are you ready to do this?" Ryan asks.

"Yep, let's get going."

We all head toward our cars to start practice.

As I put my earbuds in so that I can hear my spotter and crew chief, I take a deep breath, centering myself so that my focus is on what I'm getting ready to do.

When I pull my helmet on and hit the ignite button, the engine comes to life, and I close my eyes to take in the feeling. This rumble has always settled me. In the chaos that can be my world, this right here makes it all better.

Heading off the pit road, I see Ryan and Matt ahead of me. As I ease onto the track, I hear my crew chief over the radio.

"Okay, Mila. We are gonna take it easy on this first run. So don't go full throttle."

"Roger that."

Kicking my car into the next gear, I line up behind Ryan, with Matt to his outside.

As we round the fourth turn, I see the green flag drop as we cross the line.

Trying to get back into the groove of this massive car takes me just a little time, but I try to focus and picture what I want out of the car.

As I round the second turn and head down the backstretch, my mind races. I try to calm my breath when I hear my crew chief in my ears.

"Mila, your heart rate is spiking. Are you okay?"

Silence.

"Mila, I need you to talk to me. Tell me what's going on."

More silence.

As I reach the fourth turn, I jerk my car onto the pit road and park as soon as I'm close to my pit box.

Jerking my helmet off, I climb out of the car and storm toward my hauler.

Chapter 26
Chase

Knowing that today was a big day for Mila, I wanted to be supportive and surprise her at the track. I had spoken to Grace to get approval to come since it was a closed track while they practiced.

I had arrived at the track just as they had gotten into their cars, and I didn't want to put any extra pressure on her by knowing I was watching, so I waited back by the truck until they got onto the track and then came over to stand beside Grace.

"Hey," I say as I come to stand with her, watching the cars leave the pit road.

"How is she this morning?" I ask.

Grace looks up from her phone, smiling at me.

"She's been great this morning. And I made her do more videos than she may ever need, and she not once said no. But it could have been that she knew the quicker she did them, the faster she could get in that car as well," Grace says, laughing.

I wasn't able to catch up with Mila after she left the office yesterday. It was late when I finally got home, and Miller was making life extra hard. It's like he thinks I'm going to replace him. He had shredded his bed and took extra long on our walk. So, by the time we got back from that, I was exhausted and went right to bed.

By the time I woke up this morning, she was already on the track.

We stand by the pit wall, watching the cars take a slow lap, making sure everything is ready to go before they take them to top speed.

I gotta say, it's sexy to see my woman in her suit and behind the wheel of something that most men wouldn't even try.

As they make one last lap, I hear the crew chief tell her that this time, they will drop the green flag.

My hands are sweaty from the nerves, and I wipe them on my jeans. I try to focus on Mila. I have been worried about her getting back in the car since she had her episode in the sim lab. I know it comes to a mind-over-matter thing and it's something she has to push through, but this is her life. If she had a panic attack in the car, that could be dangerous.

I watch as she catches the next gear coming past the start and finish line and follows Ryan around the turns.

As I look up at the monitor, I see them come to the third and fourth turn. She seems to be content in her line and getting back into a rhythm. As they pass the first turn and then come out of the second, I hear her crew chief try to get her to talk to him. Her heart rate seems higher than it should be.

Shit, babe, don't do this. Calm down. You can do it.

I see her car coming down the pit road and know in the bottom of my stomach she's had the start of another panic attack.

I watch as she strips the helmet off and gets out of the car, storming off toward the hauler.

Grace turns to see what she can do, but I grab her arm.

"Let me go," I say. Grace nods, and I head to where Mila has run off to.

I get to the hauler and find Mila sitting on the floor—head in her hands and rocking just gently.

Sitting down beside her, I pick her up in my arms and cradle her as she cries ever so lightly.

"Babe, it's okay. You're safe. I have you," I tell her as I rock and stroke her back.

"Babe, look at me. You're safe," I say again, trying to get her attention.

"Chase, I can't do this. I thought I could, but I can't." She tries to look at me through her tear-filled eyes.

Sitting her up, I push her hair away from her face and cup her tear-stained cheeks.

"Yes, you can, love. You just have to find it in you again. You thought that healing your bones would automatically heal your mind. But sometimes that's what takes the longest, sweetheart."

"What if I'm never going to be ready? If I'm not a racer, then I don't know who I am. It's all I've ever wanted."

"Then you will find your way back," I say, kissing her softly and making her feel that I'm right there supporting her.

Taking a deep breath, she leans into my body as if I'm the only thing giving her strength right now.

"I need to go back out there. I need to conquer this fear and show myself that I belong."

I wrap my arms around her and stand up, taking her with me.

She wraps her legs around my hips, and I have to laugh just a little.

"Driver, if you rub against me right now, you'll never leave this hauler today. It's been a few days since I had you under me, and I'm not at all opposed to taking you right here."

And as if to test me, she grinds that sexy pussy of hers over me, making me groan just a little before I crush my mouth to hers.

A knock on the door causes me to come back to the present and what needs to be happening.

I set Mila back on her feet.

"Come in," I say just as Grace pops her head in the doorway.

"Mila, I just wanted to check on you."

"Thank you, Grace. I think I'm okay now; just had a little freakout moment."

"Are you sure? The guys were worried."

"Yeah, I'm sure. I wanna try again."

"Alright, well, come on, driver, let's get going," she says, closing the door behind her.

I pull Mila back to my chest as she walks away.

"You are amazing, Mila Michelson. Know that. And also know that I'm right here for you when you feel like life is getting to be too much."

Kissing her one more time, I spin her on her heels and push her toward the door.

We walk hand in hand toward her car. I can tell she's still tense and trying to push through the memories of what happened at Daytona.

When she looks up at me one more time, I give her a reassuring nod and wait for her to get in the car.

"You got it, driver. Now show them."

She gives me that signature smirk I love and puts her helmet on.

Walking back over to Grace, I just stand and wait.

Chapter 27
Mila

When Chase found me in the hauler, I was a complete mess. I couldn't believe he had come here. He supported me and not because it had anything to do with my recovery. He had come because he wanted to.

His reassuring words made me want to push through the block I was having and show him and everyone in that infield that I was ready to race and ready to win. So here I sit in my car, ready to go out once again.

Just as I'm putting my helmet on, I see Ryan walking toward my car.

Bending down beside my door, he looks at me, and I think I may cry all over again.

"Hey, wanna know a secret?" he says so sweetly.

"Um, sure?"

He reaches into his pocket and pulls out a penny.

"Ever wonder what the one thing is I always need with me during a race?" he asks.

I had heard the stories in the press about Ryan and Tinley, how she had given him the penny before one of the first races she attended with him, and he won. But I can't help but swoon a little, listening to him tell the story. So I don't interrupt him when he repeats it for me.

"It's this penny. Tinley gave it to me at the first race she went to with me, and it's been with me ever since. When I get stressed out or when I get nervous, I rub this penny," he says.

"Ryan, that may be the sweetest thing I've heard, but I don't think that penny is going to help me."

"Maybe not, and I wouldn't give it to you," he says, laughing. "But I just wanted you to know that even being in this sport for a few years now, I still get nervous. Hell, I've had my share of wrecks. You just have to find the thing that centers you." Looking over his shoulder, he sees Chase discussing something with Grace.

"When I met Tinley, Chase was there. Malibu Ken was what I called him. I'll never forget that day." He laughs at the name he had given Chase.

"He's a good guy, Mila, and seems to make you happy. Maybe he's your center." He stands up, clapping my car door.

"Now, you ready to run those demons out of your system?"

Nodding, I pull the strap on my helmet and get ready to do just that.

AN HOUR LATER, I'm holding my own with both Matt and Ryan as we make lap after lap, working out all the issues I've had. When we began, I had a little jitter, and my heart rate must have come across on the monitor because I heard Chase's voice as it started. His calm voice settled me and kept the attack away.

After running fifty laps, I can feel my ankle having a little pain, but I power through. I won't give up. I will just take some meds later tonight. I knew it wouldn't be easy, especially since it was the leg that I had to shift gears with. That's why Chase had me work on the rowing machine so much.

"Five more laps, Mila. Then I want you to bring it in," I hear my crew chief say over the radio.

"Roger that, boss."

When the flagman throws the white flag for our last practice lap, I feel brave and decide to put these two men in the rearview.

So when we hit turn one, I make my move.

I have been watching Matt's pattern for the last ten laps. The man has become predictable on which line he prefers, and I am getting ready to take advantage of it. I watch his car go to the top side, and I follow right along in the path, feeding off the little draft his car gives, and then I dive to the bottom.

Laughing at myself as I pass Matt, I can't help but give a brief salute as I go. Now the hard part—passing Ryan. He saw what I did with Matt, so I've lost the element of surprise. I'm going to have to put everything I have into passing him, and dammit, I am going to do it.

I catch Ryan just as we hit turn three. Ryan loves running low on the track if he can. Since I had been stuck at home all these weeks, I had taken to watching tapes and learning every move the other drivers have.

Trying to pass him on the high side, he cuts me off. So I get back in line right behind him. If I'm going to pass him, it's going to be on my terms. So I try again as we go into turn four. I push the nose of my car just to his corner panel, breaking ever so softly, and when he thinks I'm gonna drop lower, I push the car up and around him.

I reach the checkered flag, beating the teammates who have been so amazing in my recovery. But I'm also able to show them I'm still a racer no matter what the world may put me through.

"Nice race, Mila. Bring it around," my crew chief says.

As I drive down the pit lane, I can't help but smile. Today may have started out as a shit show, but it sure ended way better. Now to just put what happened behind me and get ready for the next race.

Stepping out of my car, I'm met by both Matt and Ryan.

"Nice moves there, Mila. I can honestly say I didn't see that coming. Well done," Ryan says, coming to stand with me.

"I think we may just make a winner out of you yet, Michelson," Matt says, smiling at me.

"Girl, that was amazing. Way to show these boys just how it's done." Grace comes in to give me a hug. And I think I hear a little growl come from Matt when Grace says the word "boys."

"Time to take you home, Red." Matt throws her over his shoulder, and they walk away.

"See you at the shop, Mila, and remember what I said." Ryan shakes Chase's hand as he goes toward his truck.

Chase walks over to where I stand. The man is just the sexiest nerd I could have imagined. How could you not just want to stare at him all day?

"Driver, what's got your attention?" he asks when he comes up to me, wrapping his arms around my waist.

Reaching up, I run my hand through his blond hair. I lift on my toes and give him a quick kiss.

"Nothing, just happiness is all," I say as he smiles down at me.

"Well, if you're done, then how about we go home?"

"Let me just check in with my crew chief, and then we can get out of here." I had ridden with Grace, so I don't have to worry about leaving my car at the track.

Chapter 28
Chase

Watching Mila at the track today was such a turn-on. The woman can drive a car.

When she emerged from the race car, I was amazed at the extent of her progress. It was only six weeks ago she couldn't use her leg at all, and now she's behind the wheel of a car that goes faster than most, showing her team that she's back and that she deserves to be in this sport.

Walking toward her, I just admire her in her race suit. The woman could make a paper bag look amazing, honestly. But when she's like this in her natural environment, she's beautiful. No makeup, hair in a high ponytail, and that gorgeous smile. I can't help but fall in love with her.

I shake my head as I get close to her. It's only been a few months since I first laid eyes on her. Could I really be falling for her?

"What are you looking at, driver?" I ask with a smirk on my face because I know she was watching me come over to her car. It's like a beacon guiding me to where she is.

"You were amazing out there; you know it. How's your leg feeling?"

Putting her arms around my neck, she kisses me so softly.

"It's a little stiff, but nothing that I can't deal with," she says.

Grabbing her hand, we walk toward her crew chief to make

sure everything is good for her to finish for the night. After today, I want some time with her, away from everyone.

AN HOUR LATER, Mila can finally get changed, and we can head toward home.

As we drive away from the track, Mila is buzzing with energy.

Sitting back in her seat, she finally takes a long breath and looks over at me.

"I'm so glad you came today, Chase. I didn't expect you to be there, but after my panic attack, I'm glad you're the one who was there." She looks at me as if I invented the world.

Coming to a stop at the light, I reach over and cup her face.

"Mila, when I said I was all in, that's what I meant. If you're at the track, then so am I, if you'll have me." Pulling her close to me, I give her a quick kiss as the light turns green.

"So, where are we headed?" she asks as I head down the highway toward my house.

"I'm taking you to my house. I want some time with you without having to share you. You know, just in case Grace decides she needs to visit and make sure you're okay from today."

"Sounds perfect."

As we get to my apartment building, I pull into the garage and park.

When I get out of the truck, I rush over to open the door for her and pull her into me.

Closing the door behind her, I can't help but push her against the car. I have wanted to kiss the ever-loving hell out of her since she stepped out of that car, but I've held off since I didn't want that all over the media. I still have a lot of hate for them after putting Tinley through what they did, and I don't want Mila to be subject to that.

I tilt her head just where I want it and finally take what I want from her. As our tongues collide, she grinds against me. Not wanting to miss one moment with her, I grab her leg and wrap it around my hip, hitting her at just the right angle so that if she wants to, she can get off from just rubbing against me.

Just as her moans grow, I pull away. She will not be getting herself off out here in the garage. It's going to be in my apartment with her naked and moaning against my tongue.

Grabbing her hand, I pull her toward the elevator.

Once the elevator doors close, I have to kiss her once more. I can't get enough of her.

As we walk up to my door, I'm hard as steel, and if I don't get us inside, I'm going to fuck her up against this door.

Just as the door opens, Miller comes barreling out the doorway toward me, jumping up and down like I've been gone for a month and not just a few hours.

"My gosh, who is this?" I hear Mila say behind me.

Turning my head, I see Mila smiling at the sight of my golden retriever.

Miller is the one constant in my life. The one that's here. So if he has a problem with her, then we are gonna have some issues.

Walking into my apartment, I turn to face Mila.

"This is Miller."

She walks toward us slowly, just in case he may be nervous.

Honestly, the boy has never met a stranger, and I think he would go with anyone.

She bends down to let him smell her, and the next thing I know, he's licking her face and jumping on top of her.

All I hear is Mila's laughs and her talking to him as if he were her own.

"Miller, you are such a sweet boy. Have you been good today

while Dad's been gone?" She says this like he's going to answer her.

Yep, I'm a goner. Hell, even my dog has already fallen for this raven-haired beauty.

After getting Miller settled in his kennel, I make my way back to the living room to find Mila lying on the couch, fast asleep.

Walking over to the couch, I sit down beside Mila.

I move the hair away from her face. "Sweetie, wake up."

She groans and rolls onto her back and stretches. And damn, she even makes that look sexy.

While her wrists are over her head, I grab them and lean in to kiss her.

"Tell me, Mila, would you like to have some fun?" I ask her, moving to straddle her hips.

I watch as her eyes widen just a little, and a smirk comes across her face that tells me the answer.

"Use your words, driver. I need you to tell me."

"Yes, sir."

Grabbing her off the couch, I sling her over my shoulder, smacking her amazing ass as I head toward my bedroom.

Chapter 29
Mila

Damn, Chase is hot. The moment "Yes, sir" came out of my mouth, it was like someone else took over, and it was beyond panty-melting hot.

As we enter his bedroom, I just get a quick glance. Honestly, it looks like any single guy's room. Dark curtains, matching furniture, deep-red comforter.

"So you want me to show you my world, Mila?" he says in that deep voice that has my panties getting even wetter.

"Yes, sir," I say again, but this time, I put a little sass into it. He's called me a brat more times than I can count, and I might as well play it up a little.

"Take your clothes off, Mila."

I sit up, pull my shirt over my head, and then slowly remove my leggings so that I'm only in my bra and panties.

Smirking at him, I can't help but watch him. It's like he's the hunter, and I'm his prey right now, and the more this standoff goes, the more turned on I'm getting.

"I think I said remove your clothes, Mila. You still have items on." He moves closer to me but not touching.

Moving to the end of the bed, I unhook my bra, throw it to the side, and then stand up and make a show of taking my panties off.

Chase comes to stand in front of me.

"You know, if you keep acting like a brat, I will have to

punish you, Mila." He grabs my hair and tilts my head so that I am looking at him.

"Good girls don't have fun. It's the bad ones who enjoy life," I say, just as he rubs my nipple.

"On your knees, Mila. I wanna see just what kind of trouble you like," he orders.

That commanding voice has me doing just what he asks. Dropping to my knees, I kneel at the end of the bed.

Is this what it feels like to be submissive and to be at the will of whatever is expected of you? Honestly, I am a strong woman. I didn't expect to go so willingly. Guess my subconscious likes to be submissive since my actual life has me more as the dominant.

"Eyes on the floor, driver," I hear Chase say as he steps into what looks like a walk-in closet.

Doing as I'm told, I try to get comfortable and just wait.

"Do you need a safe word, Mila?" he asks, coming back to stand in front of me.

I look up at him and notice that he's lost his shirt and is standing in front of me in low-hanging jeans, and my mouth waters at the sight.

"No, sir. I'm stronger than you think."

Reaching out, he rubs his hand down my cheek.

"Oh, sweetheart, I'll be the judge of that. Are you ready to play?" he asks.

"Yes."

"Yes, what?"

"Yes, sir."

"Get on the bed," he instructs me. As I get off the floor, I can't help but notice that he's got rope in his hand. Is he planning on tying me up with it?

I can feel my heart rate pick up, but heat pools in my middle at the idea of being tied up.

Crawling onto the bed, I'm almost in the middle when I feel a whack come down on my ass, and I let out a yelp.

"Mila, when I say get on the bed, I don't expect you to take your sweet time. So hurry, or you will get another." He steps closer.

Hurrying up to the center of the bed, I lie down on my back.

"Now, I'm gonna tie your arms and legs. Are you okay with that?" he asks, making sure that I'm comfortable with it.

"Yes, sir."

Looking around his bed, I wonder just what he's planning on tying the ropes to, and then I see the secret loops he's had put in the bed.

Once he has me tied and checks to see that my bad leg is okay, he grabs something out of his nightstand.

"Now, as I told you before, Mila, I'm more of a pleasure dom than one who just wants to bring pain."

I nod as he tells me about what he likes and doesn't like.

"If you're okay with it, I'm going to blindfold you."

I am so turned on right now. I think he could tell me he is going to pour water on me, and I would agree just to get him to touch me. I need to get off so badly, and he hasn't even done anything.

I nod my head when he brings the blindfold to my face and covers my eyes.

Chase

Never have I had someone go so willingly into this. Mila may just be the perfect partner for me.

She submits without question, and the bit of brattiness that she gives back just makes me want her even more.

When I told her about what I liked, I expected her to run, but here we are, and she wants what I'm suggesting.

Placing the blindfold on, I sit back on my knees and just stare at this beautiful woman tied to my bed.

I can play with her however I want, and I think she would let me. But that's not what tonight will be. Maybe one day, but tonight, I'm just going to show her a little of what I like.

Grabbing the vibrator off the table, I turn it on. Her head turns toward the sound.

Just as it touches her skin, she lets out a moan. She's so responsive and lets me know what she wants and when she wants more. Moving the vibrator over her nipple, she tries to move, but I have her tied just tight enough that she can't move her hips like she wants.

Kissing her perky nipple, I move the vibrator toward her clit. I know she wants to get off. I could smell her arousal when she was kneeling in front of me.

Once the vibrator connects with her sensitive bud, her hips buck, and she lets out that perfect moan. That gets me harder each time.

"Is this what you want, Mila? Do you want me to make you come with just this," I ask, playing with her nipples as I turn the vibrator up another notch.

"Oh god, yes, please, please let me come," she says between moans.

Just as I think she's getting close to coming, I pull the vibrator away.

"You come when I say so, Mila, do you understand? You only come now when I fuck you. Not with a toy," I add, making sure she hears me.

"Yes, sir."

I pull the vibrator away from her and move between her legs. As I blow a light breath over her wet pussy, she bucks on the bed.

"Please, Chase, please, I need to come," she begs—a sound that's going to play in my head for a long time.

Once I finally put my mouth on her, she's so needy. I know if her hands weren't tied at the moment, she would hold me in place and fuck my face if she could because even tied to the bed, she's trying her best to.

"Baby, lie back and let me eat my meal," I say, getting her attention.

Moaning, she finally lies back down.

"Chase, please, please fuck me. I don't know how much longer I can take this torture."

"Mila, I haven't even tortured you yet."

Mila

I feel like Chase has kept me from my orgasm for days. Even though I am sure it's not been long at all. Damn, the man knows what he's doing. He got me so close, so fast, to my orgasm, only to take it away, and now I'm on edge.

"Chase, I need to come," I growl, growing tired of him toying with me.

Whack.

"That's not how things are done now, Mila," he says as he smacks my pussy.

Damn him.

I can feel myself getting turned on even more the more he does that.

"Oh, you like that, don't you, Mila? You like it when I tell you no. You like it when I smack this wet, hot clit, don't you?" He licks it as he says it.

"Please, Chase, I can't take it. I need to come," I plead one more time.

With the blindfold on, I'm not able to see what he's doing, but the moment he gets off the bed, I feel the ropes loosen on my legs and arms.

"On your knees, Mila."

I do as I'm told and wait for what's coming.

As the bed dips, I feel his hand on my ass.

"Is this what you want, Mila?" he asks in that deep, commanding voice.

"Yes, Chase."

He slides into me so slowly I think I may combust at the seams.

Once he's pushed all the way in, we both let out a low moan.

Pulling out almost all the way, he slams back into me, nearly making me fall on my face.

Bracing for him this time, I push back into him.

"Damn, Mila, you feel so good. You take my cock so well."

Just as he picks up the pace, he pulls me flush against him, playing with my nipples as he fucks me.

He moves his hand down to my clit and pinches it, and that's all it takes. I come so fast, and my vision goes.

Letting go of me, he flips me onto my back and fucks me even harder until he reaches his own release.

"Mila," he groans out as he empties himself into the condom.

Once he's come down from his climax, he leans over me and presses my body with light kisses.

As we catch our breath, he finally pulls out and goes to the bathroom to dispose of the condom. Walking back into the bedroom, he cleans me up, throwing the towel in the hamper.

"Stay right there," he says, kissing the top of my head.

I watch him walk out of the bedroom.

Turning the covers back, I get into the bed.

Chapter 30
Chase

Walking into the kitchen, I grab two bottles of water out of the refrigerator. Sex with Mila is something that I will never get enough of. The woman is perfect.

I look over at my phone on the counter to make sure I haven't missed a message from Jasper. But what I find instead isn't something I wanted to see.

Nascar Rookie Mila Michelson is seen getting cozy with her physical therapist.

The title has me pausing, clicking the link because, of course, I'm a glutton for punishment.

Dammit.

The page opens to a picture of Mila and me at the track just a few hours ago. She had kissed me when I walked over to her after she finished practice. I wasn't even thinking of the press still being there. I was just happy for her to overcome her panic attack.

Shaking my head, I put my phone back on silent and head back to the woman who's taking up all my thoughts. That's a problem for another day. If I'm gonna be in her world, then I'm gonna have to deal with articles. Guess that's the first of many.

When I walk back into the bedroom, I find Mila curled up, fast asleep.

Pulling the covers back, I can't help but just admire the beautiful woman in my bed. She had been so receptive to the things we tried and seemed to want more.

I push the hair back from her face and try to stir her awake.

"Baby, you need to drink some water. You're coming down from the high."

Slowly opening her eyes, she gives me that smile that takes my breath away every time it's directed at me.

"Can you sit up for me just for a minute and drink some water?" I hand her the bottle as I help her sit up.

She takes a few sips before handing it back to me and snuggling back into the bed.

Placing the bottles on the nightstand, I wrap her around me. The media may have something to say about what we are, but right now, this woman is all I need, and I'll be damned if they are going to take that from me because I have a fear of being in the public eye.

When I shut my car off in front of the clinic the following Tuesday, I'm a ball of nerves. Why the hell did I have to spiral and go down the rabbit hole of pictures of us from the practice session?

Taking a deep breath, I rest my head against the back of my seat, trying to get it together before I have to talk with Jasper. Shit, he's going to have so many questions. I broke the one rule we have. Don't get involved with our patients.

But did I? When we started whatever this was, Mila had already completed her therapy. We have only been seeing each other for a little while, and we haven't put a label on it yet. She's in the process of getting ready to head to Daytona for her first race back since the wreck. Ironic that it's the same track that broke her.

I shake my head and finally get out of my car to head into the clinic for my workday.

As I'm standing at the coffee maker, waiting for my cup to finish, I feel a presence behind me. I turn to look over my shoulder and see Jasper.

Well, shit, here we go. I honestly thought I might get at least one cup of coffee before the man handed me my ass.

"Bryant, my office now," he says in his very stern Navy voice.

"Yes, sir."

Once my coffee stops pouring, I grab my cup and prepare for the talk that I didn't want to have this early but knew was coming.

"Close the door, Chase," he says.

Shit, he must be pissed. Normally, he is unconcerned about who listens to what he has to say.

After I close the door and have a seat across from him, placing my cup on the desk, he takes a long sigh.

His hair is a mess, and he looks like he's lost a few nights of sleep. Shit, this is my fault. I have fucked up royally.

Running his hand through his hair one last time, he grabs his tablet that is sitting next to his cup of coffee.

"Care to explain why the hell I'm seeing one of my trainers kissing a client?" He says this in a voice that I've never had directed at me before.

Looking down at the tablet, it's the same article that I had on my phone a few days ago. Shit, I knew I should have called Jasper the minute I saw it, but I was in such a haze from Mila that my brain said that was another day's problem. Well, looks like another day has come.

I take a deep breath and figure the only thing I can do now is tell the truth. No point in beating around the bush. He's got proof in front of his face that I'm seeing Mila.

"Sir, yes, I know this picture looks bad. But I will not apologize for it."

"Son, you know this makes my company look like we just fuck whoever comes through our doors. I have done my damndest to make sure we keep the lines very firmly in place. One picture could completely ruin all our efforts."

"I get what this picture looks like, but I was not seeing her when she was a client of ours. Hell, I didn't ask her out until I knew she had recovered."

"Tell me one thing, Chase." He stares at me, making me even more nervous sitting across from him.

"Have you fallen for this woman? Or is she just another piece of ass, and you're going to get bored after a little? Because Mac Motorsports is a big client for us, and I don't want this"—he jesters at me—"to be some, let's just have sex with a driver and see how it goes," he finishes.

"Jasper, I'm going to stop you right there before you say something that you don't want to." I can feel my blood heat the more he talks, and I've about had enough of him thinking that Mila is just sex.

"Mila is more than what you think. Over the past few weeks, I have watched that woman go from broken to cracked to healed, and I've fallen for her. She's incredible. Did I mean to fall? Oh, hell no. I wasn't looking for someone, especially someone who was in front of the public. But I guess circumstances led me to the right place at the right time. The moment she tripped into that workout room over at the race shop, she had my attention. I've tried my hardest to keep her at arm's length. But at some point, things changed, and she's now working her way into my heart, and I don't think I can get her out even if I tried.

"So no, sir, it's not about having sex with a driver. Hell, I'm still trying to wrap my brain around the fact that she wants some nerd like me anyway, but here we are." Moving to stand, I straighten up and stand a little taller.

"Now, if you will excuse me, sir, I have patients to take care of, and then I need to check on a driver."

"Be careful, son. That life isn't for everyone," he says as I go to close his door.

Damn this day. Just when I think I might adjust, I vomit the words about what I'm thinking to myself, and now that it's out in the universe, what am I gonna do?

THE WORKDAY SEEMS to drag on and on. Guess that's what happens when you have the weight of a decision on your shoulders. Just when I think I have my mind made up, it plays the highlights from the weekend, with Mila under me moaning my name, and I'm right back at square one. Guess the only thing I can do is go and talk to my raven-haired beauty.

I pull up my text chain with Mila.

> Me: Are you around?

> My Sexy Driver: Umm, yeah at the shop right now, fixing to head into the sim lab.

> Me: Wanna meet up after you're done?

> My Sexy Driver: Sure... Something I should know?

> Me: Nah, just wanting to see you.

> My Sexy Driver: Okay, I'll text when I'm done.

Walking down the hall, I grab my bag, not even paying attention as I round the corner and slam into the one person I never thought would come to see me.

"We need to talk."

When I look up, I'm hit with the not-so-happy face of Matt McCall.

"Okay," I say, motioning for him to follow me back to my office. Just fucking great. Now I'm gonna get the big brother treatment from Matt.

Dammit, Matt is one of the most relaxed drivers on the circuit, and I'm sure he saw that damn picture and has come up with his own conclusion on the topic.

"Okay, Matt, lay it on me. Just make it quick. I've had a hell of a day, and I just wanna get out of here."

"You've had a day? Far from it. I've watched my wife all fucking day do damage control for Mila. All because of you both not being able to control yourselves."

"Matt, I'm gonna stop you right there. We both know that Mila is a big girl, and she wouldn't have kissed me knowing that cameras were around. And aren't you a little of a hypocrite for coming to my place of work and trying to be all big brother for Mila? Hell, Grace acted like your 'wife' when that reporter tried to get information from you."

I step up to him… I'm so over being the nice guy.

"So before you come into my work and start trying to play the 'I'm protecting Mila card,' get your facts straight. Mila is important to me. I have no interest in being in the press. Hell, I've spent most of my day answering questions from my damn clients who saw the pictures. So how about you stay in your own lane and let me and Mila figure out just what we are? Think you can do that?"

"I just want to make sure she's okay. She's been through a lot. Grace has been with her since the wreck happened, and I don't want her to be taken advantage of because she may see you as the guy who put her back together when she was in her darkest place." He moves to the side to let me open the door.

"Believe me, Matt, the last thing I would do is take advantage of Mila."

And with that, I head toward my car to get as far away from this day as I can. But as I drive, the only place I want to be right now is with Mila.

Thirty minutes later, I'm sitting in front of Mac Motorsports.

Chapter 31
Mila

"Mila, you know you've been at this for four hours now. Don't you think it's time to take a break?" I hear Ryan say to me as he sets his own machine ready to practice as well.

"Yeah, but I just want to make sure that I have all my settings correct before we head to Daytona."

Daytona, ugh. Of course that would be the racetrack where I get to make my comeback to the racing world after my crash. The track that caused all this drama in my life.

I had spent most of the morning in Grace's office, mostly being fussed at for being so careless with that kiss with Chase, but also just having time with my friend.

If anyone can understand what I'm going through, it's Grace. Hell, her "fake marriage" played out in the media, so she knew just what to do to spin the press away from my personal life and focus back on my racing.

"Wanna race against me, Mila? Twenty laps, and the winner buys drinks at the bar close to the house?" Ryan sits down beside me, ready to race.

I had gotten a text from Chase a little while ago, and I was itching to see him. But I knew I needed to get in more time on the machine.

"You're on. Why don't you tell Tinley to meet us? Chase was just asking about doing something after I finished here, anyway. Well, unless you think that might be weird."

"Nah, I think that will be fine," he says, texting Tinley, then placing his phone next to mine.

Twenty laps later, Ryan is as smug as can be. The shithead beat me to the line by the smallest of margins, but you would have thought it was five laps.

"You know you can whip that smile off your face at any point, right?"

"Yeah, I know, but you make it so easy sometimes to get in your head. You know that, right? You had me on that last turn and then backed off just enough that I got around you," he says as we head toward the parking lot.

Just as we get to where we are parked, I notice a car parked beside mine.

"Looks like someone couldn't wait until we got to the bar," Ryan says with a laugh, heading to his truck. "I'll see you guys over there."

Walking over to Chase, I throw my arms around his neck.

"Hey, I thought I was meeting you at the bar?"

He gives me a small kiss and pulls me into his chest. When he lifts me off the concrete, I wrap my legs around his waist.

"You know, anyone could see us out here." I stare into those beautiful eyes of his.

"I don't care. I've spent more of my morning trying to figure out what we are. And honestly, the only thing I come up with is… mine."

I stare at Chase, trying to see if I heard him correctly.

"I'm yours?" I say, looking at him as if I can't make my brain say anything else.

He walks us toward his car, puts me back onto the ground, and cages me against the door.

"Mila, if you'll have me, I want to be yours. From the moment you fell into that training room, I think you took a piece of my heart that day. I have watched you go from happy to broken to panicked, and now I see that beautiful smile coming back, and I want to be the one who keeps that smile on your face. So if you'll have me, yes, I want you as mine."

Damn this man. Out of all the things that I thought he might say after seeing the pictures today, this was the last one. I was expecting him to run for the hills and never look back. My life can be complicated and requires a strong person to be a part of it, as it has so many highs and lows.

Looking up into those eyes that have shown me so much over the last few months, I become a little emotional.

Chase cups my face and presses a soft kiss to my lips. It's a kiss with the promise that he will protect me from all others and that he will take care of me. When I open my mouth, our tongues collide, and all the emotions I had been hiding away come crashing into this kiss.

Pulling away from his kiss, I stand there for a few moments, just looking at the man who has claimed my heart.

"Chase, I love you," I finally say.

When I came into Grace's office this morning, I was ready to hide under the rock that was my race car and never look back. But the more I talked to Grace, the more I understood why I wanted to act that way. I had fallen in love with Chase over the last few weeks, and then, seeing us in the pictures, I didn't want him to have to endure the media attention. He had made it known that he didn't want that. How could I make the man I love do what he didn't want all because I fell in love? But Grace had pointed out that if Chase loved me, he would accept me and my life without question. So I guess that's why I'm here standing in front of him, telling him just that.

Wrapping my arms around his neck, I say it again.

"I love you. I think I have loved you since the moment you kissed me in the treatment room and then ran away."

He cups my face and looks at me with that smirk on his face that I love so much.

"Babe, I love you too," he says.

"I just didn't want to rush you. I will wait as long as I need for you to catch up. I would have told you the moment you said you wanted to see what this was," he adds, kissing me again.

He grabs my hand and walks me toward his car.

"Ready to go meet up with Ryan and Tinley?" he asks, like this is just any other night.

I'm sure I look like a fish opening and closing my mouth. The man just said he loves me. I'm floating on a cloud. How did I get here?

Opening the passenger door, I sit down. With one last kiss, he closes the door.

As we pull up to the bar where we had our first date, I can't help but think of how much I really love this man. He's been so patient and respectful with me, and now I get to love him.

Out in the open and with all that I have.

When he pulls into a parking spot and shuts the car off, he turns to look at me.

"Mila, I'm in this. Do I dislike certain parts of your job? Honestly, yes. But after the day I've had, I would rather deal with that part than lose you because I don't want others to know about me. I will not hide in the shadows. Instead, I'll be right by your side and support you as you conquer the racing world. I want to be the man you need and the man who supports you in everything. I don't want to lose you, and I'm gonna stand right by your side as you bust through that glass ceiling."

Unbuckling from my seat, I move to straddle his lap. I don't care that we are in public or that anyone can see me. This man has just said something every girl wants to hear.

"I love you, Chase Bryant. Thank you for choosing me and being the hero in my story."

"I love you, Mila, and you definitely are the lead in mine," he says before kissing me.

A knock comes on the window a few minutes later.

"May want to stop that, kids." I hear Ryan laughing as he walks away from the car.

Letting out a laugh, we try to untangle from each other and exit the car.

"Ah, to be young and in love," Ryan says right before Tinley comes up and smacks his arm.

"What?" he says, rubbing his arm.

"Leave them alone. Not everyone has to have a dramatic event to profess their love, you know."

"Umm, I think them being in the media is an event. Hell, their picture is very similar to the way you came storming into the office recently."

I grab Chase's hand, and we head toward the bar, leaving them to reminisce about their meet-cute.

Chapter 32
Mila

Five days. That's how long I have until Daytona.

That's how long I have to make sure that both my mind and body are ready to tame the track that put me in the hospital.

After dinner with Ryan and Tinley last night, I spent the night at Chase's house. Granted, that may be why I'm on my third cup of coffee this morning, sitting across from Grace, trying to pay attention to what she's saying about my schedule for the race weekend.

"Mila, have you heard a word I just said?"

Blushing a little, I sip my coffee.

"If I say yes, can we just act like I wasn't in my head?" I say, laughing at the face she gives me.

"Ugh, you are just as bad as Matt sometimes. It's like you drivers have a one-track mind."

I have to laugh a little more at the statement because driving is the farthest thing from my mind this morning.

It's like Chase is playing on a loop in my head after what he did last night. Never in my life did I think I would be a woman who craved being submissive to a man. But my nerdy Clark Kent makes me rethink all those ideas. The more he shows me, the more I want. And let's just say that he knows how to bring me to the brink and keep me there longer than I thought possible.

"Mila, you're blushing," Grace says, bringing me back to the here and now.

"Yeah, sorry. Okay, back to the race weekend." I shake my head, ready to focus on the day ahead.

"Ha ha, okay. So, as I was saying. You have a press conference on Thursday when we get to Daytona. Of course, they will want to address the elephant in the room with the crash that happened a few months ago and how you're preparing for the race. Don't let them rattle you. You are ready for this."

I sip my coffee and listen to Grace go over the other items that I will do while at the track before qualifying on Friday and then race day on Saturday. The summer Daytona race is always a night race, which can be both good and bad. Since the race starts during the day and then transitions into night, the car is set up for night more so than day.

"Is Chase coming with you to the race? Because if so, I need to get his credentials in so he can have all access."

After we had gotten home from dinner, we had discussed his coming to Daytona, and it wasn't even a question when I asked if he wanted to be there.

"Yes, he will be with me all weekend. He's already got the okay from Jasper to leave with us on Thursday when we fly out."

"Okay, great. I'll make sure the flight crew knows he's coming and also, so I have all his lanyards ready. You sure he's ready for the crazy that's your life?" she asks, concern on her face.

"I think after the media decided they needed to know about my personal life, he saw just what comes with it. Plus, when a man tells you he loves you, there's really no going back," I say with a smile crossing my face.

"Wait. Back up. He said he loves you?" Grace asks, looking surprised that Chase said those words.

"Yep, when I left the shop last night, actually."

"Mila, I'm so happy for you. Chase is so great, and I know he is just what you need. He seems like the perfect balance in your life." She gets up and gives me a hug.

Over the last year, I have watched Grace turn from this hard-nosed bulldog in the PR world to one of the most caring and loving people in my life. I know she only lets a few people into her circle, and those are the ones who get to see the genuine hero, and I'll be forever grateful that I'm one of them.

"Okay, get on out of here. I've got a few calls to make, and you need to finish up making sure that car is ready to win this weekend." She motions me toward the door.

Three days til Daytona.

THE COUNTDOWN IS OFFICIALLY ON. As I load my bags into the back of Chase's car, it finally sinks in. I'm headed back to a track that I love but also one that took a little piece of me a few months ago. But on the other side of the coin, it brought me to Chase.

This time around, I'm gonna make Daytona my bitch and show all those who have doubted me that I deserve to be racing at this level and that I won't be backing down when they want to count me out.

"Ready to go, babe?" I hear Chase ask before closing the trunk on the car, pulling me from my thoughts.

"Yeah, let's go."

The drive to the private airport is quick, and once we park and give the flight attendants our bags, we board the plane.

Walking onto the plane, I'm hit with the memories of the last time I took this flight. I knew that going back on the track was going to be difficult, but I didn't think that every step I made today was going to be like this.

I take a deep breath and make my way over to the seats near the back of the plane. Since we are the first ones on the plane, I don't have to worry about small talk with anyone. From the way I am feeling right now, I'm actually glad to have the need to always be on time.

Chase comes to sit beside me. Just as he sits down, I can tell by his face that he knows something is off with me.

"Babe, talk to me."

Shaking my head, I give him a small smile, trying to make him see I'm okay.

"Mila, I can't help if you shut me out when it gets hard. Or did you forget I said I'm in this for the long haul?"

Just as I go to open my mouth and tell him what's going on, I hear Grace board the plane, taking my attention away from the emotions I have going on. I plaster a smile on my face and wave at Grace and Matt as they come to sit with us.

"This conversation is not over, driver," Chase says, giving me a quick kiss before turning toward Matt.

Thirty minutes later, everyone's finally boarded, and we are taxiing to take off, headed to Florida.

Putting in my earbuds, I take a nap and mentally prepare for the next few days. If getting on the plane has me stressed out, I can only imagine what being at the actual track will have in store for me.

Two hours and a little turbulence later, we land in Florida. I slept most of the flight, and when I woke, Grace sensed I needed a little space. And she doesn't bother me with all the details of what I've got going on once my feet hit the pavement.

As we go to stand, Chase grabs my hand just to give me a little comfort, and right now, that's what I need.

Once we grab our bags and load up in the van to head to the

track, Grace finally gets my attention to go over things for the weekend. And damn, did she pack a lot of items into it?

"Okay, once we get to the trailers, I need everyone to get changed, and all three drivers are going to have a press conference. As Mila is making her comeback in this race, and it is a restrictor plate race, we must show the press that we are a united front and function as a team. That we aren't individual players.

"Then next, we will have a small meet and greet with some local kids who are up-and-coming stars around the area.

"After that, you are welcome to have your own personal time. Until tomorrow, and then we will start it all over again."

She hands out a piece of paper that has every hour mapped out to the tee on what's going on this weekend and where I am needed.

"Damn, Red, did you block off any cowboy time on this damn paper?" Matt says, catching Grace's attention and the eyes she just gave him. Let's just say I'm glad I didn't bring up the hour-by-hour time clock. But yeah, I was thinking the same thing.

"Guess if I want time with you this weekend, I'm gonna have to steal you away, babe," Chase whispers in my ear, making goosebumps break out all over my skin.

"I'm sure I can arrange that," I say, giving him a smirk of my own.

"If I had it my way, I would have you in my hauler right now and not let you leave until I was coming on your tongue."

I'm pulled from my very private conversation with Chase by someone's throat clearing; turning to face said person, I'm met with the same eyes that just got a hold of Matt. Well, damn, now I'm in trouble too.

Chapter 33
Chase

Day one in Daytona, and I'm already exhausted. Hell, we haven't even been here for eight hours, and Mila has already put in more of a workday than most people would ever do. I'm sure we have walked the length of this track five times now with the back and forth we have had to endure. But watching her in her element, it's been the best sight.

The woman knows just what to say to have the press eating out of her palm, and not once has anyone asked about her personal life and the physical therapist. That alone has me riding a high right now. They are solely focused on her race weekend, how her car is, and the teammates she's come to know as family now.

As she finishes up with the meet and greet, I'm standing back against the wall, just watching her talk with the younger girls who are looking at her like she hung the moon, when that familiar scent hits my nose.

"You know, you two are pretty perfect for one another. She brings out the side of you I didn't know you had," Tinley says playfully, pushing my shoulder as we stand and watch Ryan and Mila talk to the kids.

"She makes it easy. She makes me want to be something different. I didn't think I wanted this world, you know, being in the media. But Mila makes me want to deal with it all. She's my world, that's for sure, and it happened when I wasn't wanting something serious."

"That's how it happens. You know, when I went to the race and met Ryan, I wasn't looking for him. He just found me, and the rest is a kind of history. We may have never been endgame, Chase, but look what it brought us to. One encounter sends you into another world, and then you find the love of your life," Tinley says, smiling at Ryan as he walks toward us.

"See you tomorrow, Chase," she says as Ryan grabs her hand, and I watch them walk toward the exit.

Standing against the wall, I give it a few more minutes while Mila talks with another young girl, then I make my way over to her.

As I walk up behind her, I wrap my arms around her waist, unable to stop myself. I have watched her all day, and now it's finally my time to have her to myself.

"Ready to go, driver?"

Letting out a sigh, she turns around in my hold, and I'm hit with the chocolate eyes that bring me to my knees.

"Let's go." She links our hands, and we head toward her hauler.

The pit area is finally quiet after all the press and spectators from earlier, and the moment we hit the drivers-only area, she finally lets out the breath she had been holding since we left the meet and greet.

"It's been a long day, babe. How's your leg feeling? With all this walking and up and down, I know you have to be hurting, even if it's just a little." I'm a little concerned that she may have overdone it.

"Really, my leg is fine. I think I'm exhausted from the day itself. I forgot just how much goes into race weekends," she replies as we get to her hauler, and she walks up the steps.

As we step into the hauler, I cannot help but be in awe of her. She's a female racer in a male-dominated sport. Coming back from the injury she endured, she was ready to still take on the pack again. She's stronger than she will ever know, and I'm damn proud of her.

"What are you thinking, Chase Bryant?" she asks, pulling me out of my thoughts.

Stepping up to her, I need to kiss her. But I take my time with the kiss, not rushing or making it urgent. It's one of love, slow and possessive.

"I love you, Mila Michelson," I say, pulling her into my chest and breathing in the smell that is just Mila.

"I love you more, Chase Bryant," she says, wrapping me tighter in our embrace.

"So tell me, driver, what is your race day ritual? I need to know what gets you ready for the race time."

"Ha ha, honestly?"

"Yep, I wanna know. I don't want to mess anything up. I'm sure you're a superstitious bunch, and I wanna make sure everything goes perfectly for you."

"Well, how about we make a new race day ritual?" She wiggles her eyebrows at me.

"What did you have in mind, driver?"

Chapter 34
Mila

Racers are all about routine—Chase is right about that.

Drink the same drink if you had a dominant race.

Eat that snack bar you did when you qualified a spot ahead of your rival.

Listen to a certain playlist if it gets you in the right headspace.

Well, after the last race at Daytona didn't go as I had hoped, this time, I'm changing that up, and having this gorgeous man in front of me just might be the first change in that.

Looking up at Chase, I feel my cheeks heat, and he gives me a smirk as if he can read my mind.

"Do you want to play, driver?" he asks in that commanding voice.

"Yes, sir."

"On your knees; I want you to suck my dick."

Slowly lowering to the floor, I try to rub my knees together to help ease the ache that is building.

He begins to unzip his jeans and lower his boxers, making his dick springs forward. I lick my lips, wanting to taste him.

Just as I go to open my mouth to take him, he grabs my hair, drawing my attention up to him.

"Now, Mila, I didn't say you could start yet, did I?"

"No, sir," I say, knowing that I'm in a little of a brat mood tonight, and I wanna see how far I can get before he punishes me.

"You have far too many clothes on for my likes. I want you naked when you take me in your mouth."

Removing my clothes, I sit back on my knees, once again waiting for him to tell me I can have what I want.

I'm so turned on that I rub myself without even thinking. I need to find some release.

"Dirty girl, are you trying to get off sitting on your knees?" Chase says as he watches me.

He walks up to me and tilts my head up.

"Open your mouth, Mila, and show me just what you want, and I might even let you have more than me just fucking your mouth."

Doing as I'm told, I work Chase over and over until I feel his balls tighten and his release coming.

I keep a hold of him and swallow every drop until he pulls back.

"Damn, Mila, you take my cock so good," he says, rubbing some of the dribble that's left on my mouth over my lips.

"Tell me, Mila, what other ritual do you want to do?" he asks me, getting back to the reason I started this little game.

WAKING THE NEXT MORNING, I'm a little sore in all the right places, to say the least. This new race ritual is one that I will definitely use even if I have a terrible race. It was just as much fun for me as it was for Chase.

I stretch and pull the cover off, only to be pulled back by the powerful arms of my love.

"Ugh, do you have to get out of bed? I enjoy having you naked beside me."

I push him onto his back and straddle his hips, rubbing against him one last time just because I've turned into a needy girl, and I can't help myself.

"I have to get ready to head to the last practice before qualifying." I rub against him one more time, making us both moan.

"Babe, if you keep that up, I'm going to fuck you hard and fast just to show you I'm still in charge, even though you are trying to show otherwise right now."

Leaning back just so slowly, I lower myself down on him inch by inch. Damn, this man and his magic dick.

I ride him slowly, seeing if he will let me take what I'm so desperate for.

As I pick up my pace, he grabs my hips and pistons into me, harder and harder. Within a few minutes, I'm coming all over him, and he lets go of his own release, filling me with everything he has.

It's not until I've come down that I realize we didn't use a condom. Shit, we haven't had a conversation about this. We have always been safe. The one time I was reckless and let my lady parts take control.

"Mila, look at me. You're safe. I know what you're thinking. I'm clean. I haven't been with anyone since I knew I wanted you. And before that, I always wore a condom."

I nod my head, trying to wrap my mind around what he's saying. I have an IUD, so I don't have to worry about getting pregnant, and I've never had sex without a condom either, so why am I freaking out?

Bending down, I kiss the man who knew I was having a freakout moment and took the time to make sure I was okay. Chase Bryant has my heart for forever if he wants it.

"Thank you, love you."

"Love you too, babe, and just for the record, if you want to wake me up like this every day, I wouldn't be opposed to it," he says, smacking my ass as I move off him and head toward the shower.

After taking a shower and trying to get my head in what is expected of me today, I finally emerge from the bathroom.

When I walk into the living area, I see Grace talking with Chase, who is now dressed, and damn, those Clark Kent glasses are hot every time I see them on him.

"Okay, that's enough of that, Mila. You're already late, and I can only hold the press for so long," Grace says, grabbing my to-go coffee from Chase as I give him a quick kiss goodbye.

Following Grace toward the garage area, I look over the agenda for today. It's lighter than yesterday, thank God. We have a short practice cycle then qualifying today.

Once we get to the garage, I finally relax a little. This is the place where I have always felt at peace. The smell of motor oil and gasoline. It does something to my soul, and I know I'm home.

I take a deep breath and walk over to my crew chief, who is getting the car ready to go for later. Once I make sure he needs nothing else from me, I head to my next aim.

The drivers meeting.

Heading into the meeting today, I knew I would get looks. Most of the guys knew I was coming back today. But I think a few wondered if I would be back to one hundred percent. Well, joke's on them because this driver is back, and she's ready to show the boys who they need to fear this weekend.

"Over here, Mila," I hear Ryan say over the crowd that's talking around in smaller groups.

"Overwhelmed yet?" he asks with a small laugh.

I can't help but give him the side-eye as I go to sit beside him while we wait for Matt to join us.

I swear, if it weren't for Grace, that man would be late for literally everything. It's like he just gets lost and can't find his way if she's not directing him.

When he finally joins us, I laugh at the shape he is in. It's like he ran the length of the track to get here.

"Problems this morning, man?" Ryan asks, trying to hold back his laughter at his best friend.

It's hard to make out the small grumble that comes from Matt, but it sounded a little like, "I'm gonna punish my wife later."

Once the drivers' meeting begins, the room falls silent, allowing everyone to pay attention to what is expected of us at both qualifying and the race tomorrow.

Just as the meeting is finishing up, the chairman points out that I'm back this weekend.

"I wanted to welcome back Mila Michelson this weekend. It's been a long road to recovery, but we are happy to have you at the race this weekend, Mila," the chairman says as he claps.

Fuck me. Why do I need to be the center of attention? Can I just not be like any other driver?

I smile and thank him, then stand to head back to my trailer and get ready for qualifying.

Three hours later, qualifying is finally over.

Honestly, I thought I was going to have a panic attack as soon as I strapped into the car, but it went better than I expected. Partly because I could run by myself and also because Chase was with me, keeping me calm while I ran my laps.

Now we have established the running order for the night race.

Ryan placed fourth.

Matt placed eighth.

And I ended up fifteenth.

Which honestly isn't terrible, but it isn't the best because that just means I have to start in the middle of the pack. Being in the middle on some tracks is great, but it's not so much at this track.

The middle is where the wrecks happen. Guys try to push when they don't need to or get past being happy and end up sending you around just because they get impatient.

I ensure everything is set for tomorrow as I get out of my car and head to my hauler so I can go to bed.

Just as I'm walking toward the driver hauler area, I'm met with a reporter.

Damn, I really thought I might get away from having to answer questions tonight, but I guess my luck has run out.

"Hi, Mila. James, from MRN. Mind if I ask a quick question?"

Taking a deep breath, I breathe a little easier. At least he's a NASCAR guy and not some random person with a podcast.

"Sure, go ahead," I say, putting a smile on my face that Grace would be proud of.

"With being back at Daytona this weekend, do you think you're mentally prepared to tame this track after the serious wreck you had here just four months ago?" he asks.

I feel Chase with a comforting hand on my lower back, and I take a calming breath.

"I think I'm as ready as I can be. I've put in the time and the hours to get back to the level of the race. I've had an amazing support system that has pushed me but has also taken care of me. So, yeah, I'm ready."

"Thanks so much, Mila, and good luck tomorrow. I'm sure you have tons of little girls rooting for you and can't wait to see what you will do in the coming weeks."

"Thanks, James. Have a great night," I say as Chase grabs my hand, and we walk to the hauler.

Just as we make it there, Chase spins me so I'm facing him.

"You know you're pretty incredible, Mila. You impress me with how easy you make things look," he says, pressing a kiss to my lips.

"You're pretty great yourself, Chase."

"Come on, let's get you to bed. You have a race to win tomorrow."

Chapter 35
Chase

Saturday morning at Daytona.

I wake up earlier than I should have, but my nerves are on high alert, and I can't shake the worry that's in my stomach.

Loving someone is scary. Loving someone who gets in a car and goes over two hundred miles per hour on purpose. That's a whole new level.

Needing to clear my mind, I leave Mila to sleep and put on my running shoes. It feels different not having Miller with me this weekend while I'm here, but I know he's living his best life with my parents. They sent me a picture last night of him lying at the end of their bed like a king.

The sun is just coming up when I make my way to the track. Maybe if I can get in a few miles, I'll be able to relax and not let her see that I'm a ball of anxiety with her getting back on the track today. I need to be the one who shows her she can do this.

By the time I make my way back to the hauler, I've cleared my head of some of the worry and can think somewhat straight.

Walking into the bedroom, I see that my heart is still fast asleep. So I strip down and jump in the shower before I wake her up for the day.

By the time I'm finished, she is already up and making coffee when I come into the living area.

"Morning, babe." I move to kiss her on the cheek before grabbing my cup of coffee.

"Where did you go this morning?"

"Just needed to go for a run. Clear my head a little. Watching you in this environment honestly has me on edge," I tell her.

She walks over to me, wraps her arms around my middle, and rests her head on my chest.

Kissing the top of her head, we just stand like this—breathing in the last few moments with one another before she's pulled away to get the day started.

SIX HOURS LATER, the race is only two hours from going green.

Mila has been going from one press conference to another meeting to a quick signing since she stepped out of the trailer. So I'm glad she's finally able to take a break before the race and rest.

"How's the leg feeling today, babe?" I ask, making sure she's not overdoing it, considering she's going to drive in a few hours.

"Feels good. A little stiff in the ankle area, but nothing I can't deal with."

"Have a seat, and let me see if I can loosen it up a little. I mean, what's the point of having a boyfriend who's a physical therapist if you don't use me?"

Once I have her shoe off, I can look at her ankle, and yeah, it is a little swollen from all the walking that she's done over the last few days. It's not terrible. Once I have her do a few motions with it, she seems to relax.

I ice it for about thirty minutes before putting some heat on it to help the joints a little more. Then I decide that we need to wrap it so it's a little more stable, and that will keep the swelling from getting worse while being in the car for the entire race.

Mila

Race days are one of my favorite things. And today has been no different.

After Chase checked on my ankle and made me keep my leg elevated for a little, it was finally time to get up and get ready for the race.

Pulling on my fireproof suit and making sure my hair is secure, I'm ready to head to the car.

When I look over at Chase, I can't help but fall more in love. Damn, every time I look at him.

Giving him a quick kiss, we head toward the track.

We walk hand in hand. I've got my pods in, listening to my track playlist, which I have listened to since I could drive. It always puts me in the headspace I need to get ready.

A few little girls stop us as we head to the car, and I can't help but grin at the joy that lights up their faces from just speaking with me. I remember being their age and wondering why there weren't women drivers out there. So I went and became that driver the little girls can look up to.

Chapter 36
Mila

Saturday, Daytona Night Race...

Walking up to my car, I hand Grace my ear pods and get focused on the race.

Both Ryan and Matt come by and check in and wish me good luck tonight.

As the national anthem plays, I can feel Chase looking at me as if I'm going to shatter into a million shards of glass at any second.

"What's wrong, Chase?"

"Nothing, babe. I just want you to know how very proud of you I am, and no matter the outcome of today, you've won," he says.

As the song stops and we are told to get in our cars, I can't help but pull Chase close to me.

"Chase Bryant, I love you with everything I have. Thank you for pushing me to get back here and for staying by me, even when I wanted to push you away."

Cupping my face in his hand, he says, "Mila, I would have waited for as long as I needed for you, and I will always be here. I love you more than all the races you will ever run."

"Now kiss me and go show them how it's done."

And that's just what I do. Media be damned, this man owns

my heart, and if the world needs to know anything, well, then they can ask.

Strapping into my car, I dial in for what needs to happen tonight. I'm already in the mindset that it's okay if I don't win. Hell, I just want a top-ten finish. My goal tonight is to finish with my car in one piece and prove not only to myself but to all those who say women don't deserve to be here that we do.

"Drivers, start your engines," comes over the intercoms.

Cranking the car, it comes to life, and my vision instantly goes blurry.

"Mila, you okay?" I hear my crew chief ask.

As I shake my head, trying to come back to what's happening, my eyesight levels out, and I take a deep breath.

You can do this, Mila—mind over matter. You've driven a race car a million times, and it's no different. Show them what you're made of.

"Yeah, I'm good," I finally say over the radio, feeling my mind click into place with what I need to do today.

"Okay, let's have a good race, and Mila, you deserve to be out there. Show them what you're made of," my crew chief says as he goes quiet, and my spotter comes onto the radio.

"Alright, Mila, we have four hundred miles ahead of us. Let's ease into it, and then we can see where the pack goes. One hundred and sixty laps can make for a long night at Daytona, so take a deep breath and be ready to go when they drop the flag." I slowly move forward in the lineup, getting ready to make our first laps under caution before the green flag drops.

Three laps later, we are making the last turn to head toward the front stretch. Kicking my car into a higher gear, I get ready to hit the gas and start the race that I have been working toward for over six weeks.

"Go, go, go," I hear my spotter say, and before I second guess myself, I hit the gas.

Stage one goes by in a blur. All I focus on is getting the rhythm back and making sure that if I have anything that needs to be adjusted when pit stops come up, I can tell my crew.

Just as I'm coming out of turn four and heading toward the line, my heart rate picks up, and it's like slow motion coming at me.

Two cars ahead, I see the forty-four spin, and all hell breaks loose.

"Low," my spotter says just as the car in front of me gets hit.

I'm bobbing through the cars and smoke, trying to figure out just which hole I can get in to make it out of the mess.

"Take the grass, Mila. That's the only hole you have to get away from the carnage."

Pushing my car down off the apron and into the grass, I hit the gas and plow through the smoke.

When I emerge, I see a clear track ahead of me and finally let out the breath that I had been holding in.

"Great job, Mila. I knew you could do it."

"Mila, are you good? How does the car feel?" I hear my crew chief come over the speaker.

"Yeah, I'm a little shaken up, but I think the car is good," I tell him.

"Bring it in under caution. Let's check. Since you had to take the grass, I want to make sure none got into the underside of the car."

"Coming around now."

Once I pull into the pit box, the team rushes out to inspect the car and make sure I've got enough gas and a fresh set of tires on before giving me the green light to head back out. Brandon, my IT guy, makes sure that all the screens are working and providing the correct readings since they had wanted to short out a little in practice. But they seem to be back to normal.

"Did Matt and Ryan make it through the wreck?" I ask.

Since they were a little ahead of me, I wasn't sure where the wreck had actually started position-wise.

"Yeah, both are good. They were a few cars ahead. So our job now is to try to get the three of you together if you're up for it."

"Sounds like a plan."

It takes what feels like forever for the crews to get the cars cleaned up, and then five caution laps later for us to get back to racing.

When the green flag drops, I have one mission.

Get to Matt and Ryan and show everyone in NASCAR that our team is one to look at this year.

ONE HUNDRED LAPS IN, and I have busted my ass to make it to Matt. It seems like every time I get close to him, someone decides they wanna play bulldog and test my patience. Well, guess what? I've officially run out. The next person who comes at me like I don't have a clue how to drive—I'm sending them straight into the wall. I've reached my point of no return.

Turn three comes into view, and I can see Matt's bumper pushing my car just a little extra. I finally made it to the fifth spot.

I give Matt a little tap just so he knows I'm here and that I'll be locking in behind him. Ryan is running in the second spot, and I think with me pushing him, we can make it to Ryan. We just have to be smart about it and time it just right.

"Mila, about damn time you joined the party. What took so long?" Matt says over the radio.

"Really funny, Cowboy. Now you wanna make my life easy? Am I gonna have to carry you to the front?"

"Let's go then."

And with that, I kick my car into the next gear, pushing Matt forward as we come out of turn four.

Thirty laps to go in the Coke 400.

The last thirty laps are always the ones I either love or hate. With the big wreck already happening, the field is less, but you always have to keep your guard up. The last few laps are the ones where drivers get ants in their pants and think they can literally drive through you, so you have to keep your focus on everything.

After a few laps, Matt and I finally reach Ryan, and now we find ourselves locked in what appears to be a train.

Ryan has the fastest car out of our group today, so it was only fitting that he's the lead car in our line, putting him in second place.

I was just trying to keep my panic from rising with each passing lap.

Things have gone a little too easy for us since the major wreck that almost took me out, so I was just waiting for something to happen.

"Mila, when we get to lap fifteen, I want you to slingshot past Matt," I hear my crew chief say over the radio.

"Why? His car has been significantly better than mine all day."

"I just spoke to his crew chief, and they are worried he may be low on gas by that point, and if that happens, he's gonna have to drop out of line. So he knows you are gonna go around him on that lap and attach to Ryan."

"Okay."

Following Matt for the next few laps, I get anxious about the what-ifs. But I remember what Chase said to me before getting in the car.

As I come out of turn two and head down the backstretch, I slingshot past Matt and make room between him and Ryan.

I know my car is on point today, but Ryan's is just a little better, so if I can't get the win, he sure as hell will.

Chase

I have paced the length of this trailer all night. I tried to stay in the pit area and watch from the box, but my legs wouldn't stay still.

So now, here I sit, watching Mila's race on the TV.

I am so damn proud of my girl for overcoming her fear and doing what she loves. When she made it through that massive wreck, I knew she would be found and that she had her head where it needed to be. When she pulled into the pit box under caution, and the team checked on her, and she gave a thumbs up, she was back to being the high-speed adrenaline woman who first caught my attention.

Five laps to go, and Mila is in third place right behind Ryan, with Matt still behind her. I heard over the radio that Matt may be low on gas and that's why he and Mila swapped spots, but he's held on so far.

I try to watch on the screen, but I can't stop walking the length of the trailer yet again.

When they round the fourth turn, I go back out to the pit box with the team.

Just as I'm heading down the steps, I see Tinley step out of Ryan's trailer.

"Couldn't stay in the box, either?" she asks with that bright smile that I loved all that time ago.

"Little too much media for my liking."

"Yeah, that's why I normally stay away until the race is almost over. I don't need them catching all my emotions in one go."

"Come on, we only have a few laps left, and your guy may just win this thing if Mila has anything to do with it."

As we get close to Mila's pit area, Tinley waves by and heads to Ryan's, which is only a few down from us.

It's amazing the way things end up like they do. Tinley could have been my endgame, but a racer changed that, and now a racer is who I see as mine. Funny how that happens.

By the time I get to the box, it's two laps to go, and Mila is pushing Ryan as they come out of turn three. All she needs to do is keep him in front of the eighteen cars, and they can win this one.

By the time the white flag drops, I honestly don't think my heart can take another lap. Mila has pushed Ryan into the first spot and is now sitting in the second right behind him.

I knew going into today that Mila was something special with driving, but holy hell, the woman can compete with anyone you put against her.

The white flag flies for the last lap. Just four turns separate her from showing the world that she's back and ready to challenge anyone who doubted her.

Chapter 37
Mila

Holy shit. White flag.

Four hundred miles at Daytona and one major wreck. I've done it.

I've shown drivers, crews, press, and all the fans that I deserve to be here. That I can come back from being shattered and broken to rise and prove to those who doubted me.

Finally, I give Ryan one final push, sending him toward that checkered flag with me right behind him.

"Way to go, Mila, awesome race!" I hear my spotter come over the headset.

Going around Ryan, I throw my hand out the window to congratulate him as I make my lap around.

Today may not have been my day to win, but hell, I'll take a second to someone who I know deserves it and that I helped.

Today was about showing not only myself but all those little girls that you can do anything as long as you work hard for it.

My wreck those months ago didn't define me as a driver or as a woman. That wreck revealed that I was capable of something beyond my expectations.

The moment I woke up in that hospital bed, I wanted to crawl into a hole and never come out. But Grace made sure that I never felt like I wouldn't get back here. Yeah, I may have made it hard sometimes, and being a grump didn't help.

But I think the moment Chase saw me broken and helped

put me back together, my life clicked into the place where it needed to be.

It's funny how life can work like that. If you had told me a year ago that I would have been in a crash, broken my leg, and would be driving and coming in second a few months later... I would have thought you had taken something.

So maybe falling that day in the training room started me on the path that brought me here. That brought me to the love of my life.

Pulling into my pit box, I see the crew standing on the wall, all with smiles so wide, like we won the race. And I guess, in some ways, we did. I didn't have a panic attack this time, and I came in second to my teammate.

I spot Chase before I even get out of the car. He is standing over by himself, smiling that dimpled smile with his Clark Kent glasses on. Not rushing to be in the middle of it all, just letting me have my time. And I fall in love with him all over again. We may not have started out the way others fall in love, but I guess sometimes the love of your life just might be the one you didn't even know you would need to put you back together.

Epilogue
Chase

12 Years Later...

"Cole, will you get your jacket on? We're going to be late," I tell my eight-year-old son just as he speeds past me on his bike.

"Dad, Alex isn't even ready yet," he says as he makes yet another lap on the BMX track we had made in the backyard.

I swear that boy is the reason I already have gray hair.

Letting out a sigh, I turn and head toward the house to see if Alex, our ten-year-old daughter, has decided that today she's gonna be my sweet child and not choose violence like I've gotten the last few days.

"Alex, are you ready?"

"NOT YET, DAD!" she yells from her bedroom.

"You realize that she's going to choose violence over being sweet, right?" Mila says as she comes around the corner, putting her jacket on as she laughs.

The woman gets more beautiful with each passing year. I knew I wanted to marry Mila Michelson from the moment she stumbled into the gym that day, and with a lot of tries and even more effort, she finally became my wife eleven years ago.

She still races now and then, yet her love now is being in charge of the driver development at Mac Motorsports and getting to be home each night with our kids.

"Alex, will you just come on?" Mila shouts to our daughter, which gets her coming out of her bedroom.

"Finally, what the hell took so long?" I ask, which gets me the side-eye from my wife and a growl from my daughter, these two are the same person I swear.

"She's making sure she looks pretty for Landry," Cole says, coming in the back door like the whirlwind he is.

Crossing my arms over my chest, I look my daughter in the eye. I try to see if she'll give up any information herself, but the girl is like Fort Knox and not giving me anything.

Looking over at Mila, I see her grinning ear to ear.

"And does Tinley know our daughter has a crush on her son?"

Throwing her hands in the air, Alex makes yet another sound only dogs can hear and storms toward the car.

Over the years, we have stayed close to Ryan, Tinley, Matt, and Grace. Then, when we all started having kids, I guess it was just a matter of time before things shifted. But damn, I'm not ready for my daughter to have her first crush.

"Cole, get your ass in the car. I think you've said enough for today."

After what takes far longer than needed, we finally head to the regional airport. I promised Jasper we would stop by and see the exhibit his son Ash was traveling with this weekend, hoping the kids might enjoy another form of speed today that wasn't a stock car.

Ash was a part of the famous Angels and is now commander of the new group that tours the country for demonstrations.

I was able to see him fly a few times during his tour when the Angels would appear at the races when Mila was driving.

Parking the car, we make our way over to Jasper, who's already talking with Ryan and Matt.

"Can't be on time at least one day, can you, Bryant?" I hear Jasper say as we approach them, standing by the gate.

"You try to get a ten-year-old to dress quickly and not lose a body part," I say, laughing as Alex gives me the death stare.

I watch as Mila talks with Tinley and Grace while Jasper goes over the events for the day, and I stand back and marvel at the life that I've been given.

Mila took a chance on me and never looked back, and I fell in love with that fiery spirit and drive that makes her so perfect.

The life we've built is one that I didn't expect to have, especially with the media wanting to know every aspect of our lives, but it's one that I accepted, and I wouldn't change it because it brought me here.

"Whatcha thinking, Bryant?" Mila asks, wrapping her arms around my neck just like she did all those years ago, and it makes me want to live in that time all over again.

"Just taking a moment."

Giving her a tender kiss, I pull back just slightly so that I can take in those eyes that held me captive all those years ago.

"Thank you. I don't think I ever said that."

"What are you thanking me for?" My statement puzzles her.

"For taking a chance with us and giving me your heart, Mila. I told you I would protect it with everything that I have, and I think we have built a pretty amazing life together. And I can't wait to see what the next twenty years bring."

Kissing her one last time, we make our way over to our friends, who are now family, and start the next twenty years. Driving into the sunset.

THE END

Acknowledgments

And with that, book three and the Driving Series has come to a close. When I started writing Ryan and Tinley, I never thought that I would be hitting the end on book three. But here we are, and I am so excited for everyone to read Mila's story. I hope some see themselves just a little bit in her.

To my husband Ereck, thank you for helping with the NASCAR information that I needed to make sure was right. I know you thought I was crazy when I asked questions sometimes but you always laughed and still helped. An I love you so much for supporting me along the way.

To Annie Charme, thank you for reading over my words if I ever needed and extra set of eyes and helping with scenes that needed just a little something.

To Ethan, thank you for helping with the physical therapy part of this book. You may have thought I was joking when I ask for your help earlier this year but as you see it was needed.

To my beta readers, Kelly thank you so much for reading over my story and letting me know where I needed more sassy Mila or those swoon worthy moments for Chase. I have loved the process with you in my corner.

To Cadwallader Photography—Katie, thank you so much for the beautiful image and for helping pick the one that worked perfectly for Mila - Y'all make sure to check her out for all our cover models. So here's to the next one coming soon.

To Marley Williams, thank you for being the face of Mila Michelson. And being a part of this process, for being so sweet when I bugged you, letting you know I was going to be tagging you—a lot.

To Samantha from Sammie Bee Designs, thanks for bringing my cover to life yet again. I love it more each time I see it. Who would have ever imagined being a reader, one day, I would ask you to bring my cover design to life? I couldn't have asked for a better partner in this adventure, and both covers are beyond anything I could have asked for.

To Kat's Literary Services (Steph & Louise y'all are amazing), thank you so much for putting up with me and editing my story. You make me a better writer. I'm so glad you took a chance on my writing. I have loved working with you and having you all in my corner.

To the readers…thank you for taking the time to read my story. Being a reader first, I know you have so many options for what to read; if you chose mine, I am forever grateful. I know the story may not be perfect, but for this baby author, I'm so glad you wanted to read it.

To all my writer friends thank you for being in my corner and supporting me with anything I may have questions on or just being a friend when I need to vent

To Christine (Concepts by Cane-a) you are such as amazing artist and I can't shout your images to the masses enough. Thank you for making the best images of my characters and for becoming such an amazing friend and sounding board. Even when you draw something and I end up having to write a Christmas book because of it :) Y'all make sure to check her out and get some fun images from her!

Becoming a writer wasn't something on my radar, but I've just started writing. Book three has been a work of love, and I'm so glad that the words finally came together and you have them in your hands now. Enjoy! Haley

About the Author

Hi, everyone. I'm Haley (some of you may know me as The Southern Librarian in the book community). Married to my best friend, I'm the mother of two teen boys. I grew up in small-town North Carolina and still live there now.

Racing has been in my blood my whole life; my dad taught me how to count using race cars and then took me to tracks when I was a little girl. I met my husband at a local dirt track. So it's easy to see that I would write a NASCAR trope.

Stay tuned for what's to come, and I hope you enjoy this ride with me. I never thought being a writer was something I would be able to achieve or share my stories, but one day, I started writing, and these books are the product of that one day.

DRIVING SERIES

DRIVING Force

Ryan & Tinley's Story
Order Now:
Driving Force

DRIVING Wild

Matt & Grace's Story
Order Now:
Driving Wild

DRIVING
Heart

Mila & Chase's Story

Order Now:

Driving with Heart

DRIVING Force

Want to see how Tinley & Chase first met…
Check out Chapter One of Driving Force.

DRIVING *Force*

HALEY COOK

Chapter 1
Tinley

"Y'all–I DO NOT WANT TO GO!" Ignoring my protest, I'm thrust into the shower. "You're going–kicking and screaming if that's what we have to do," Mia declares. Having been my best friend since freshman year at App State, she knows when it's time to get me out of the house. "You need a day out away from books and working at that library surrounded by more books. It's your last year. Enjoy college for a change."

What's wrong with liking books? I think to myself.

"Tin, I know what's rolling around in that little head of yours, and yes, books are fine, but you need other things in your life. Like boys and boys and more boys," she points out.

"Mia, you know I'm the girl who is invisible to boys or the one they friend zone, right? I may be the quiet girl, but I'm not as shy as some may think. I just don't let people get too close because I don't want my heart broken."

"That's where you're wrong, Tin. You just don't let them see you and the awesome person you are because you have read so many romance novels that no man can ever live up to that idea of the perfect partner."

It's easy for her to say. Her dark brown hair, big blue eyes, and curvy figure make the boys stop and take notice anywhere we go.

"Ugh. Okay, fine, I'll go." I give in, but my less-than-pleased tone makes my reluctance very clear.

Living with my best friends for the past three years, I understand that we usually have the most fun when they get me out of my comfort zone. Mia, Grace, Lily, and I might be very close, but you build a complex quickly when you're the single girl and everyone else is coupled up. I can't help if I get lost in my studies more than hanging out with the six of them. My Saturday nights usually consist of the girls getting ready for dates and me reading the latest book on my Kindle instead of being the seventh wheel.

And yes, I know what you're thinking - *Don't they have hot friends to set you up with to go along with them?* The answer is yes, they do, considering they are all dating guys on the baseball team. But their guy friends always seem to see me as the chubby girl who makes them laugh, not girlfriend material. Don't get me wrong, they have all been super sweet, but it's always the same thing. "I like you, but I just think we are off as better friends." So, it never goes further than the first date.

If they are dragging me to God knows what today, I better put some effort into it, or I'll, as my mother says, *die alone with a cat*—by the way, I don't even like cats—then it'll eat my face off. Since I'm alone, no one will find me until it's too late. Insert face palm emoji here, please.

After finally pulling myself out of the shower and drying off, I'm met with three pairs of eyes staring at me like I'd just said I was Team Jacob instead of Team Edward.

"Umm, ladies, what's up?" I no sooner get the last word out before different clothing options are thrust at me like I've never dressed myself before.

"Okay, let's slow down. Of course, I have some questions. First," I lift my hand, "where are we going? And second, why are all three of you so excited about this?"

Lily is the first to chime in. She's usually the quieter of the four of us, the normal southern girl. Auburn red hair, dark green eyes, and the sweetest personality you will ever meet. Even if she told me she planned to kill me in my sleep, she's so sweet I wouldn't believe it until it happened. This explains how she landed James, the star baseball player, two years ago. We are all sure she'll follow him to whichever farm team he lands at after the draft in a few months.

"Ok, so don't kill us, but we're going to a NASCAR race," Lily tells me, a little too excited for my taste.

Pausing to let it sink in a little, I finally reply, "Umm, y'all know I like quiet places, right? I mean, I work in a library and want to go into publishing when I finish school. In what universe did you think this would scream, 'Hey, Tin will love this and will put up no struggle whatsoever about going?'" I ask, looking at them quizzically.

"Yeah, yeah, we know you like boring," Grace chimes in.

Yes, Grace is that friend, that bitchy girl that will always say what she thinks even if no one wants to hear it. She has blonde hair, green eyes, and wears her signature red lipstick, ready to cut any man who might impede her because she gets what she wants.

"But guess what, Tin? You're going! I pulled some strings, and a family friend who does PR for a team is letting me get some experience for my PR/Social Media class. He got us all passes to the Food City 500 Race in Bristol, Tennessee since it's only an hour from here."

Knowing I don't really have a choice, I shrug. "I better get dressed, then. Yee haw, make me a NASCAR pit lizard, I guess. Show me what I've been missing all these years."

None of my friends find my sarcasm or exaggerated Southern accent funny. Instead, they pounce on me like lions in the jungle that just found their last meal. When they finally give me an inch of breathing room, I turn to look at myself. The dark colors of the royal blue fitted tee and dark-washed jeans enhance my curvy figure, but my favorite part is the signature sparkly chucks that I always wear.

"Let the games begin, bitches!"

Grace does her Breakfast Club fist bump in the air. Lily stands back, jumping and clapping, and Mia just shouts, "Hell yeah, you are smoking hot!"

I don't know about smoking hot, but I feel better than average with my hair done in loose curls and a little makeup applied. The humidity living in North Carolina can be rough, so it's best to just go natural.

Going to a race might be the craziest idea known to man because I know I'll be out of my element. But my girls have all the confidence in the world, making me smile and hold my head higher. Just as we walk into the living room, a knock comes from the front door. Lily heads toward it like she has a beacon on James and knows his every move—but I've always been told that it's the quiet ones you've got to watch out for.

James no more gets his foot in the door than I realize I'm once again the seventh wheel. Lily and James are so cute it would make anyone sick. When James settled down, his buddies wanted that same thing, so that's how Mia and Grace fell for his best friends. Here I sit, a single girl in a room full of couples. Then, out of the corner of my eye, I notice a guy I haven't seen before trailing behind Miles. Granted, it's hard to see around Miles. Standing six foot three and built like a linebacker, he takes up a lot of space. James is the shortest of the bunch by a few inches. It's hard not to look at them and see why my best friends are lucky women. Internally kicking myself for being so picky. Great, not only am I going to a sporting event I know nothing about, but now I'm being set up on a blind date. Yep, where is the wormhole I can jump in?

"Okay, are we ready to go? I need to see what the huge deal is with NASCAR."

Miles, Grace's boyfriend, is the first to chime in. "You're going to love it, Tin. Fast cars and beer. What's not to love?"

"Miles, you know me so well." *Just kill me now,* is what I really mean, but I give him a playful smile.

The next thing I know, James is pushing a handsome man with blonde hair and light green eyes in front of me. If I were a betting woman, I'd say this is one of his athlete friends based on his build alone.

"Tinley, this is Chase, and no, he does not play any sports before you even ask. Well, not at school, anyway. I know you're tired of athletes. Even though I should be hurt by that, I'm not. He's in my sports medicine class."

"Hi, Tinley." Chase reaches out to shake my hand. "It's nice to meet you. James has told me a lot about you. Thanks for letting me tag along to the race today."

Lordy, this man is nice to look at. His sea-green eyes could make a girl lose all train of thought and whereabouts when his attention is on them. Maybe it won't be such a bad day after all. "It's nice to meet you, Chase. I would love to say that James and Lily have also told me all about you," I laugh a little, "but they didn't. I'm so sorry."

"Well, if I had known that James had such a beautiful friend, I would have made sure he had given me your contact sooner." I can't help but blush at the statement. Chase may just be what I was looking for, or maybe he could help me figure out this racing shit my friends thought I needed to understand.

As we follow the others out and load up into Miles's suburban, I tell myself to just enjoy today. Even if it kills me. And between NASCAR and a blind date, it just might.

Want more of Ryan & Tinley's story
Grab your copy now.

Available on Amazon & KU

HALEY COOK

Driving Force